THE YARMOUTH TRAIN
BY
MALCOLM WHITE

The Sea & Land Heritage Research Series
2005

INFORMATION

Published by Malcolm R. White   Printed by Micropress Printers Ltd.
              Coastal Publications   27 Norwich Road
              71 Beeching Drive   Halesworth
              Lowestoft   Suffolk
              NR32 4TB   IP19 8BX
              First Published June 2005   ISBN 09547323 2 4
              Copyright © Malcolm R. White 2005   All rights reserved

Every effort has been made to ensure the information contained in this review is accurate and for this reason many sources of information have been consulted. These include personal accounts of events, official documentation, local diaries, media resources, and numerous accredited research works. However, when considering such a complex, varied and historical subject, 100% accuracy cannot be guaranteed. By popular request, all measurements, dimensions and distances in this book are stated in British Imperial. Books in this series are part of the National Published Archive and as such are included in the library collections of the British Library, the National Library of Scotland, the National Library of Wales, the Universities of Oxford and Cambridge, Trinity College, Dublin, and when appropriate, The National Museum of Science & Industry. Unlike the majority of publications, this book is not produced for commercial gain for the author or publisher, profits from the series are donated to railway charities and other good causes.

OTHER TITLES IN THIS UNIQUE SERIES

DOWN THE HARBOUR 1955-1995	40 years of fishing vessels, owners, the harbour and shipyards at Lowestoft	ISBN 09532485 0X
A CENTURY OF FISHING	Fishing from Great Yarmouth and Lowestoft 1899-1999	ISBN 09532485 18
FISHING WITH DIVERSITY	A portrait of the Colne Group of Lowestoft	ISBN 09532485 26
CROWNIES OF LOWESTOFT	The steam trawler fleet of Consolidated Fisheries	ISBN 09532485 34
DRIFTING, TRAWLING & SHIPPING	A portrait of Small & Co. (Lowestoft) Ltd.	ISBN 09532485 42
GREETINGS FROM LOWESTOFT	A picture book of old postcards and photographs	ISBN 09532485 50
THE LOWESTOFT TRAIN	The railway at Lowestoft and scenes on the lines to Norwich, Ipswich and Yarmouth	ISBN 09532485 69
LOWESTOFT ANTIQUITY	A picture book of once familiar scenes	ISBN 09532485 77
THE BOSTON PUTFORD STORY (1)	Fishing and Offshore Support from Great Yarmouth and Lowestoft	ISBN 09532485 85
LOWESTOFT CORPORATION TRANSPORT	Lowestoft Trams, Buses and Bygone Town Scenes	ISBN 09532485 93
RAILS TO THE COAST	East Anglian Seaside Stations, Sheds and Rail Links– Great Yarmouth and Lowestoft	ISBN 09547323 08
A DIFFERENT LOWESTOFT	Some Missing Features of a Grand Old Town	ISBN 09547323 16

PHOTOGRAPHS

Front Cover (Top) - A rare 1970 colour view of the Yarmouth South Town-Lowestoft line just prior to closure showing a hybrid dmu at Gorleston. (PK)
Front Cover (Bottom) - A scene from September 1958 showing Gresley designed Class B17/6 4-6-0 No. 61656 *Leeds United* at St. Olaves with a train from Yarmouth South Town. St. Olaves station can be seen in the background. This locomotive entered service in 1936 and was withdrawn for scrapping from March depot in January 1960. *(EA/CR).* **Title Page** - A stopping train for Yarmouth South Town leaves Woodbridge in an impressive way behind Class B17/6 4-6-0 No. 61668 *Bradford City*. This engine was completed in April 1937 and cut up at Stratford in September 1960. It was the last of the class and would have been a superb candidate for preservation, no examples of this well known type have been saved. A busy station, Woodbridge is now served by the Lowestoft-London through trains. *(JH/EMJ)* **Opposite Page** - One of the two streamlined Class B17/5 4-6-0s, Norwich allocated No. 61670 *City of London* hard at work in 1950 on the East Suffolk line whilst heading a Yarmouth South Town - London Liverpool Street express. *(JH/EMJ)*

CONTENTS

	PAGE
INFORMATION	2
ACKNOWLEDGEMENTS	4
INTRODUCTION	5
THE RAILWAYS OF GREAT YARMOUTH by the late Mr. K. A. Frost	7
STATIONS IN THE TOWN	
Yarmouth Beach	18
Yarmouth South Town	34
Yarmouth Vauxhall	48
SCENES ON THE RAIL ROUTES	
Yarmouth-Lowestoft-Beccles	60
Yarmouth Beach-Melton Constable	69
Yarmouth South Town-Ipswich (Direct)	78
Yarmouth-Norwich Routes	90
COLOUR SELECTION	97
YARMOUTH RAILWAY MEMORIES	105
THE RAILWAY TRAMWAY	107
PHOTOGRAPHIC INDEX	116

ACKNOWLEDGEMENTS

Much appreciated has been the assistance and support offered during the preparation of this book by many kind people dedicated to researching and recording local railway history and those who have offered their photographic collections for use in this book so that others can enjoy their work. These include in particular, Mr. Stuart Jones BA, who has provided editorial support for the many titles in this popular series. Assisting or participating in this complex project have been The Pendragon Partnership, Stephanie Berry, Mr. Peter Calvert, Mr. A. E. W. Colbourn, Mr. D. F. Cole, Mr. Norman Fairhead, Mr. Peter Killby, Mr. Barrie Laughland, Mr. Geoffrey Moore, Mr. Peter Parker, Mr. Terry Reeve, Mr. Colin Tooke, Mr. Peter Snell, Mr. David White and Mr. Steffan White. Finally, I thank my wife Cathryn for the patience, support and understanding she has shown during the very long hours I spend writing, publishing and distributing books in this series.

I am indebted to Mrs. June Frost for allowing the use of her late husband's work in this book, and also to Mr. Michael Blakemore for allowing the use of material previously published in the **Back Track** magazine.

PHOTOGRAPHIC OWNERSHIP AND COPYRIGHT

For a great many years South Town was considered the gateway to Great Yarmouth from London and the presence of a Britannia Class 7MT 4-6-2 locomotive at the station was considered normal. Class member No. 70030 *William Wordsworth* rests at the sheds whilst waiting a return to London Liverpool Street with the fast service "The Easterling", having arrived earlier with the down train. The two cylinder Britannia locomotives were introduced in 1951 having been designed at Derby. (PK)

INTRODUCTION

Living close to the Norfolk and Suffolk Joint Railways Committee line and Lowestoft North station, meant than from 1952 until 1964 trips by rail to Great Yarmouth were very frequent for me and, from 1964 until 1970, became a daily commuting event. The great attraction of Great Yarmouth for the "train spotter" or railway enthusiast were the three stations, each with different types of locomotives to suit the services the stations provided. A further railway attraction, the unique quayside railway always provided a fascinating sight as the train made its way through the town centre road traffic, over the bridge approach and along the quay to various locations including quayside sidings, depots, scrap yards and the Fishwharf. Unfortunately, car drivers frequently obstructed the track by leaving their vehicles on or near it, causing operational difficulties in later years. With government approval for a new harbour and ferry terminal to be constructed in the foreseeable future near the port entrance, one wonders if it was wise to close this direct rail link from the port area to the national rail network and in recent years remove all the track.

In the 1950s, Great Yarmouth's most important railway station was perhaps considered to be South Town with the fast direct route to London Liverpool Street. Locomotives to be found at South Town were large steam and diesel locomotives needed for the through services and smaller locomotives required for local services to Beccles and Lowestoft. Beach station was the most easterly of the three and always had a unique attraction since it was one of the few stations in East Anglia where Midland Region locomotives could regularly be found. The station provided a wide selection of services to the Midlands and the North and special trains to Scotland in the autumn and winter.
Vauxhall station, now the only remaining rail terminus in the town, has always been considered somewhat inconveniently placed. It has handled cross country services, the many Norwich local services and some London trains, although this pattern has changed in recent years. As a station at the end of a local line from Norwich, a limited number of locomotives and types were to be seen at Vauxhall, however there was the occasional visitor from the Midland Region with a through working.
Goods and freight traffic including coal, wood, bricks, cattle, grain and salt was handled at the various stations in considerable amounts, especially during the annual herring fishing season when coal for the steam drifters and salt for packing fish was in great demand. Frozen food was also dispatched by rail from South Town and Vauxhall stations. Today (2005), no rail freight is handled at the town's station. Great Yarmouth was at one time considered the best rail served medium town in the UK and was a truly great place to visit for the railway enthusiast. It is one of the largest and most popular holiday resorts in the UK and a substantial port. Despite a reduction in the number of through services that now serve the town, it remains a major destination for vast numbers of rail passengers .

This book, which has been compiled following numerous requests, compliments two other railway titles "The Lowestoft Train" and " Rails to the Coast", both of which include information and many photographs of railways around Yarmouth, Gorleston, and the local area. It has been a pleasure to record and highlight some of the past railway heritage of Great Yarmouth, in this, the first comprehensive book ever to review this important location.

Whilst images highlighting the age of steam predominate in this book, to cater for the rapidly increasing interest in diesel traction and the modern network, many scenes of Yarmouth Vauxhall services intentionally feature diesel motive power.

Malcolm White
June 2005

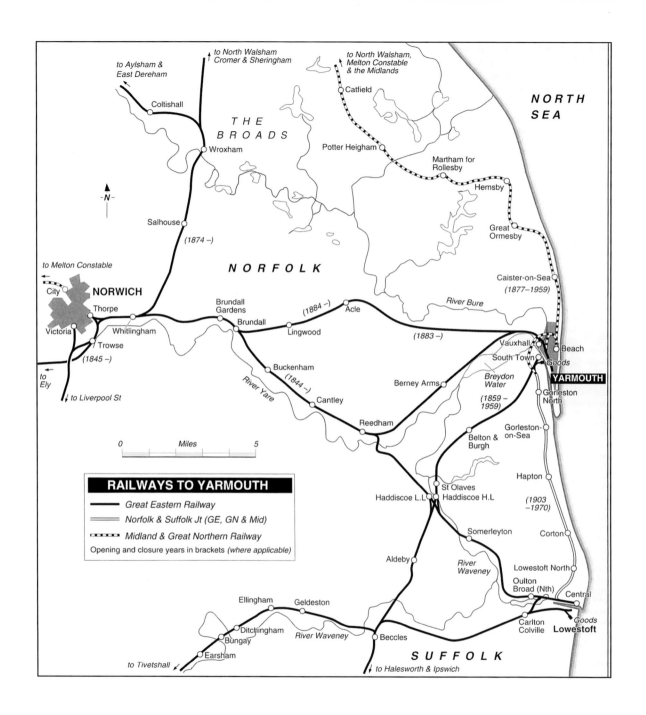

to Aylsham &
East Dereham

to North Walsham
Cromer & Sheringham

to North Walsham,
Melton Constable
& the Midlands

NORTH
SEA

Coltishall

THE
BROADS

Catfield

Potter Heigham

Wroxham

Martham for
Rollesby

Hemsby

Salhouse

NORFOLK

Great
Ormesby

(1874 –)

to Melton Constable

City

NORWICH

River Bure

Caister-on-Sea
(1877–1959)

Thorpe

Brundall
Gardens

Whitlingham

Brundall

(1884 –)

Acle

Victoria

Lingwood

(1883 –)

Vauxhall

Beach

Trowse

South Town

Goods

(1845 –)

YARMOUTH

to
Ely

Buckenham

River Yare

(1844 –)

Berney Arms

Breydon
Water

Gorleston
North

to Liverpool St

Cantley

(1859 –
1959)

Gorleston-
on-Sea

Reedham

Belton &
Burgh

Hapton

RAILWAYS TO YARMOUTH

St Olaves

Haddiscoe L.L

Haddiscoe H.L

(1903
–1970)

——— Great Eastern Railway

Somerleyton

Corton

Norfolk & Suffolk Jt (GE, GN & Mid)

Midland & Great Northern Railway

Opening and closure years in brackets (where applicable)

Aldeby

River
Waveney

Lowestoft North

Oulton
Broad (Nth)

Central

Ellingham

Geldeston

Carlton
Colville

Goods

Ditchingham

Lowestoft

Bungay

River Waveney

Beccles

Earsham

SUFFOLK

to Tivetshall

to Halesworth & Ipswich

0   Miles   5

-N-

6

The Railways of Great Yarmouth
by
The Late Mr. K. A. Frost

Prior to the coming of the railways, all goods arriving from the sea for Norwich or being exported from that city had to be tran-shipped at Yarmouth which involved the payment of harbour dues at that port. Discontent among Norwich traders concerning the level of these charges led to proposals for the establishment of a way to the open sea through Lake Lothing, a move naturally opposed by Yarmouth which spent £8,000 in mounting opposition to the Bill when it came before Parliament. However, the Admiralty, being anxious to make Lowestoft a Harbour of Refuge, supported Norwich with the result that the Bill received Royal Assent on 28th May 1827 authorising "the making and maintaining of a navigable communication for ships and other vessels between the City of Norwich and the Sea at or near Lowestoft in the County of Suffolk".

The New Cut as it became known (i.e. the Ship Canal 2¼ miles long connecting the Waveney and the Yare) was opened on 30th September 1833. Yarmouth suffered as a result and also because steam navigation had reduced the time for the conveyance of goods to London, while Norwich initially found that coal prices remained high.

It was shortly after this, in December 1834, that the prospectus of the Grand Eastern Counties Railway was issued, outlining plans for a trunk route commencing from a terminus to be located in Shoreditch High Street and proceeding by way of Chelmsford, Colchester, Ipswich, Eye and Norwich to Yarmouth, at 126 miles the longest line then projected in the United Kingdom.

Following surveys by John Braithwaite and C. B. Vignoles, it was claimed that it would involve no major engineering works, no tunnels or viaducts, with embankments limited to a height of 30ft and the steepest gradient 1 in 400. Among the many advantages claimed for the proposed railway was that fish traffic would be increased tenfold and Yarmouth and Harwich reinstated as leading ports for the Continent and northern Britain. (A branch to Harwich was to be provided later).

The Eastern Counties Railway ("Grand" had been dropped from the title) was incorporated by an Act of 4th July 1836 with an authorised capital of £1,600,000 in shares of £25 and £50.

Having decided to begin work at both ends of the line simultaneously (it being considered that the London/Chelmsford and Norwich/Yarmouth sections held out the best prospects of a quick return on capital invested), financial difficulties and incomplete land purchase negotiations prevented a start being made at the Norfolk end and operations began on the London/Chelmsford section only in March 1837.

While the directors favoured the gauge of 7ft 0¼ ins being adopted by Brunel for the Great Western Railway, Braithwaite (who had been appointed engineer) managed to persuade them to agree to 5ft, an unfortunate decision since the tracks had to be converted to 4ft 8½ins after only a few years in 1844.

The Eastern Counties Railway encountered endless difficulties, especially with rapacious landowners and by the time the line had been completed to Colchester in March 1843, the 51.2 miles had cost the company £600,000 in land and compensation alone. The actual construction, including track and engineering expenses having accounted for £1,631,330, had absorbed more than the total estimated for the construction of the entire line from London to Yarmouth and the scheme had to he curtailed at Colchester.

The inability to proceed beyond Colchester confirmed what had been anticipated for some considerable time and it led to disappointment and chagrin among the citizens of Norwich and Ipswich. Such was the feeling in Norwich that a meeting was held in that city on 21st January 1841 under the Chairmanship of Lord Sondes to consider the possibility of an independent railway to London. A proposal for linking Norwich and Yarmouth by rail as an initial move was formulated.

The Eastern Counties powers to build the line between Norwich and Yarmouth having lapsed, that company intimated its intention to apply for a renewal of its original powers but the Yarmouth & Norwich Railway Bill received Royal Assent on 18th June 1842, the Eastern Counties securing certain clauses protecting its interests. At a meeting ten days later, George Stephenson was unanimously elected Chairman of the company while Mr. William Fothergill

Cooke was present to explain the working of Cooke and Wheatstone's electric telegraph which it was decided would be provided for the line.

The Chief Engineer of the Yarmouth & Norwich was Robert Stephenson and G. P. Bidder was also engaged, the contractors being Grissel & Peto who commenced work in April 1843. There were no major engineering works involved and the formal opening of the line took place on 30th April 1844 when some 200 guests travelled on the first train that left Norwich for Yarmouth at 10.30am. The return journey to Norwich was performed in 44 minutes and a dinner followed in the Assembly Rooms. The line opened for public traffic on the following day, the service comprising four trains each way and another celebratory dinner took place at Yarmouth that same night. The railway was single track throughout. Fares for first class were 3s 6d, 2s 6d for second, and 1s 3d for third class, cheap day returns being issued at 5s, 4s and 2s respectively.

Intermediate stations were provided at Brundall, Buckenham, Cantley, Reedham and Berney Arms. Signalling was extremely primitive a lofty pole at the end of each platform being furnished with a basket painted red. If this was pulled up to the top of the pole the train was to stop. Semaphore signalling was unknown on the line but on the other hand, the telegraphing of a train's progress was in advance of any system in use on any other railway at that time.

The Norfolk interests were still very much concerned with establishing a route to London and a further scheme was formulated to build a railway from Norwich to Brandon where it was planned to join the projected line of the Eastern Counties Railway from Newport in Essex. This had originally started as the Northern & Eastern Railway, authorised on the same day as the Eastern Counties, for a main line from London to Cambridge and had reached Bishops Stortford on 16th May 1842. On 1st January 1844, the Eastern Counties took the Northern & Eastern on a 999 year lease and, Parliamentary powers having been obtained already for an extension to Newport, secured an Act on 4th July 1844 to extend the main line from Newport to Brandon with a branch from Ely to the London & Birmingham Railway at Peterborough. The Norwich & Brandon Railway Act had secured Royal Assent two months previously, on 10th May.

The Yarmouth & Norwich (Y&N) amalgamated with the Norwich & Brandon on 30th June 1845 to form the Norfolk Railway and exactly one month later, on 30th July, the 36¾ mile double track Trowse - Brandon line of the newly-termed Norfolk Railway was opened, together with the Brandon - Newport line of the Eastern Counties Railway, thereby establishing through rail communication between London and Norwich via Cambridge, Ely, Thetford and Wymondham. On 15th December 1845, the completion of the Trowse swing-bridge enabled entry to be made into the Norwich terminus and, by means of a junction linking up with the Y&N line, through running to commence between Yarmouth and London, the best times being six hours up and five hours 40 minutes down. Meanwhile on Wednesday 8th January 1845, a public meeting had taken place in the Town Hall at Great Yarmouth about the proposed London & Norwich Direct Railway. This concerned a proposal for a main line from a junction with the Northern & Eastern Railway at Elsenham, proceeding in a north-easterly direction to Bury St. Edmunds and then continuing via Ingham and Barnham to Thetford, there to join the Norwich & Brandon Railway. The total length was 45 miles ten chains and the overall distance from Yarmouth to London by this route would have been 128 miles, against 143 by the route via Cambridge and Ely then nearing completion.

At this meeting the report of a committee appointed at a previous public meeting to consider the several railways proposed to he connected with Yarmouth (e.g. the Diss, Beccles & Yarmouth scheme of 1845 and its successor, the Waveney Valley & Great Yarmouth Railway, neither of which materialised) recommended the public "to concur in and forward by every means in their power the London & Norwich Direct Railway as being the shortest distance from Great Yarmouth to London and opening a communication with an extensive and populous part of the country hitherto having little commercial dealings through the port of Yarmouth" and it requested the member of Parliament for the borough to support such a line in Parliament. Although the report was unanimously received and adopted, the company got no further than issuing a prospectus.

Meanwhile, the first seaside hotel in Yarmouth, the *Royal,* had been built near the beach in 1840; Dickens stayed there in 1848, four years after the opening of the Yarmouth & Norwich Railway. Between May and September 1846, Yarmouth recorded 80,000 visitors arriving by rail, as well as many more who had come by steamer from London. Considerable development took place in the ensuing years and by 1858 the Marine Parade had been completed, Wellington Pier had been built and a second pier, the Britannia, was being erected.

The coming of the railway to Yarmouth facilitated better and faster distribution of fish and then, in 1847, a 1¾ mile street tramway was opened to the quay area from the goods station. In 1867, an extension to the tramway was constructed to the new Fishwharf. This new facility was officially opened in February 1868 and greatly improved fish landing and selling facilities; the arrival of the railway had already resulted in the bloater becoming available to ever larger numbers of people.

Yarmouth had to wait fifteen years until 1859, before its second railway, which was to provide it with a more direct route to London, was opened. In these years, the Eastern Union Railway, formed by the citizens of Ipswich initially to link their town with the Eastern Counties Railway at Colchester, had reached Norwich with its own independent terminus (Victoria) on 7th November 1849, which led to the original station being named Thorpe. Shortly after this, in 1851, the Halesworth, Beccles & Haddiscoe Railway was incorporated for the purpose of linking the river ports of Halesworth and Beccles to the Reedham-Lowestoft line of the Norfolk Railway which had been opened some four years previously. The contractors were Peto, Brassey & Betts and the line was brought into use on 4th December 1854. In the meantime, the Norfolk Railway had been empowered to make a working arrangement with the new company but it was the Eastern Counties which operated the railway since it had taken over the working of the Norfolk Railway in 1848.

By this time the East Suffolk Railway had been incorporated on 3rd July 1854, taking over the powers of the Halesworth, Beccles & Haddiscoe to continue the line to Woodbridge, to which town the Ipswich & Bury Railway had secured an Act some seven years earlier authorising an extension from Ipswich. Implementation of this latter scheme had been delayed due to financial reasons.

In 1856, Peto promoted two small nominally independent companies, the Lowestoft & Beccles and the Yarmouth & Haddiscoe, to link up with the East Suffolk Railway's system. He immediately leased both companies for 21 years at 6%. These two small companies were amalgamated with the East Suffolk Railway in 1858. Incidentally, Peto actually considered promoting a main line from the Eastern Union Railway at Colchester to Pitsea on the London, Tilbury & Southend Railway (of which he was a lessee) to establish a completely alternative route from Yarmouth and Lowestoft to London.

The contractors for the entire line from Ipswich to Lowestoft and Yarmouth were again Peto, Brassey & Betts and the engineer George Berkeley, who had designed Fenchurch Street station. While devoid of any engineering works of an outstanding nature, the East Suffolk line certainly presented its share of problems, necessitating many curves and involving a gradient profile resembling a switchback. Work began in 1856 and on 4th March 1859, Capt. Tyler of the Board of Trade carried out his inspection of the main section of the line from Woodbridge to Lowestoft and Yarmouth, followed by another inspection two months later of the Eastern Union Railway's extension from Ipswich to Woodbridge (the Ipswich & Bury Railway, the original promoters of this line, had been absorbed by the Eastern Union as from 1st January 1847 and amalgamated with it six months later).

The line was opened throughout on 1st June 1859 to a new terminus in Yarmouth at South Town, it was double track throughout although the Lowestoft branch was single track. The principal celebrations took place in the latter town where a banquet was given by Peto, a special train from Bishopsgate reaching Lowestoft in 3¾ hours, which was considered very good. Among the distinguished guests were the Chairmen of the East Suffolk Railway, the Eastern Counties, the Eastern Union, the East Anglian and the Norfolk Railways.

The initial passenger service comprised three up and three down through trains to and from London and one local train in each direction on weekdays; two up and two down through trains were run on Sundays.

Very shortly after this the Eastern Counties Railway (which had worked the East Suffolk from the outset) together with the other nominally independent railways in East Anglia were amalgamated to form the Great Eastern Railway by an Act of 7th August 1862. The best journey time from London to Yarmouth had now come down to four hours 35 minutes via Ipswich and in 1863, the 1000am express from Bishopsgate was scheduled to cover the 121¾ miles in three hours 25 minutes. However, this proved very taxing for the locomotives and the timings had to be eased so that it was not until 1880 that such a schedule re-appeared in the timetables.

In 1876, a short line that was later to become part of the Midland & Great Northern Joint Railway was sanctioned. This was the Great Yarmouth & Stalham Light Railway authorised as a light railway under the provisions of the Regulation of Railways Act 1868. It was 17¾ miles long and the contract was given to Wilkinson & Jarvis. The Yarmouth terminus of this line was in Nelson Road North, about 200 yards from the north beach and convenient for some of the principal hotels. The first section of this railway, to Ormesby, was opened on 7th August 1877 and it was extended to Hemsby in May of the following year when the company obtained a further Act authorising an extension from Stalham to North Walsham, a distance of seven miles, and changing the name to the Yarmouth & North Norfolk Railway. The line was eventually opened to Stalham on 3rd July 1880 and was single track throughout with many level crossings. The train service was six each way daily and three each way on Sundays. By the 13th June 1881, the line from Yarmouth had been extended to North Walsham. Yarmouth therefore, now possessed three railway stations, Vauxhall, South Town and the new terminus which from 5th April 1883 was known as Beach.

Meanwhile the first serious steps had been taken elsewhere in the building of what was eventually to become an important route linking Yarmouth to the Midlands. In 1866, the Midland & Eastern Railway was constituted, formed by the amalgamation of a group of lines west of Kings Lynn, the Norwich & Spalding, Spalding & Bourne and Lynn & Sutton Bridge. Later on, the Lynn & Fakenham was opened on 16th August 1879 as far as Massingham and completed to Fakenham a year later. The Lynn & Fakenham then completed its system to Norwich, opening as far as Guestwick via Melton Constable on 19th January 1882, to Lenwade in the following July and reaching Norwich on 2nd December. It now only remained to forge the link between Melton Constable and North Walsham to complete a through route from Yarmouth to Kings Lynn and beyond, and this section was completed and opened on 5th April 1883. By this time, the Yarmouth Union Railway had been authorised on 26th August 1880. Despite its somewhat ambitious title, it was a very short line of one mile two chains built to connect the Beach station with the quayside tramways of the GER. It was opened on 15th May 1882 and shortly afterwards was amalgamated with the Yarmouth & North Norfolk and the Lynn & Fakenham to form the Eastern & Midlands Railway. The Yarmouth & North Norfolk had ceased to be a light railway under the terms of the Act, which it had obtained jointly with the Lynn & Fakenham on 11th August 1881 authorising the Melton Constable to North Walsham link. Six months after this first amalgamation a

second one took place when the Midland & Eastern and the Peterborough, Wisbech & Sutton Bridge also came into the Eastern & Midlands. Thus, this newly-formed company now had an unbroken system from Bourne and Peterborough to Norwich and Yarmouth.

On the original line from Yarmouth (Vauxhall), the growth of traffic led to the decision to build a more direct single-track relief line from Brundall to Yarmouth via the small town of Acle. This line (which reduced the distance by rail between Norwich and Yarmouth by two miles) was opened for traffic from Breydon Junction to Acle on 12th March 1883 and the remaining section to Brundall on 1st June the following year.

In October 1892, the Great Northern and the Midland Railways reached an agreement on terms for the absorption of the Eastern & Midlands Railway and that a Bill should be drawn up to authorise this. This led to the creation of the Midland & Great Northern Joint Committee by an Act of 9th June 1893 and the Eastern & Midlands was vested in the new undertaking with effect from 1st July 1893. The offices at Kings Lynn became the committee's general offices.

In 1897 the Great Eastern and the Midland & Great Northern Joint Committee, having decided to co-operate regarding certain extensions to their systems in Norfolk, reached agreement on the setting up of a new committee, the Norfolk & Suffolk Joint Railways Committee, to control certain railways which it was proposed to build with a view to developing traffic on the coast, among them a line from Yarmouth to Lowestoft from a junction at Gorleston. This new venture was to have four directors from the Great Eastern and four from the Midland & Great Northern (i.e. two each from the Great Northern and the Midland). The Act establishing this committee received Royal Assent on 25th July 1898. Prior to this, Parliamentary sanction had been secured by the Great Eastern on 3rd June 1897 to build the Joint Committee's Yarmouth - Lowestoft line and a few weeks later the Midland & Great Northern had obtained powers for the Lowestoft Junction Railway to link the Norfolk & Suffolk Joint line at Gorleston with its station at Yarmouth Beach, a 3¾ mile line involving the building of a viaduct over Breydon Water and the crossing of the Bure, the Norwich road and the Great Eastern lines from Vauxhall and South Town. The actual Norfolk & Suffolk Joint line commenced at Gorleston North Junction and joined the Great Eastern at Coke Ovens Junction, a short distance from Lowestoft Central station. At the Yarmouth end, the Great Eastern' s link line ran from Gorleston North Junction to South Town station. To connect with its station, Yarmouth Beach, the Midland & Great Northern link necessitated the construction of the Breydon Viaduct, 800ft long with four fixed spans and also a double swing span on a central pier to allow for the passage of shipping. Single track only was provided on this viaduct which was the principal engineering feature in the building of the Yarmouth - Lowestoft line, making the whole enterprise expensive since the viaduct alone cost £67,000. In the construction of this short coastal railway, no fewer than twenty three bridges had to he built and five stations were provided, Gorleston North, Gorleston-on-Sea, Hopton, Corton and Lowestoft North. By early summer 1903, the line had been completed and on Wednesday 8th July it was inspected by Major Druitt, the Board of Trade Inspector. During the course of this inspection, six heavy locomotives were coupled together and sent over Breydon Viaduct which was found to he satisfactory. The railway was opened on 13th July, the first public train from Lowestoft to Yarmouth Beach leaving at 8.37am and connecting at the latter point with the 9.20am express to the Midlands and the north. Extensive alterations and improvements were made to Beach station in anticipation of increased traffic.

The railway system at Yarmouth was now complete and was destined to remain intact for over fifty years during which time it contributed greatly to the town's role as one of the principal holiday resorts in the country and also as the centre of the herring industry. Until World War I the bulk of traffic inland was carried by rail. Through expresses to and from the Midlands had begun to be operated by the Midland & Great Northern in July 1894, being initially confined to the summer months only. The trains became known as the 'Leicesters' (although they also served Birmingham) and were later improved by being provided with through carriages to Derby and Nottingham. In October 1902 the service began to be operated all year round and at Derby it was possible to make connections to Liverpool and Manchester and similarly at Nottingham to Sheffield.

The Great Eastern, meanwhile, was also running through trains between Yarmouth, Lowestoft and Cromer and the Midlands and the north. In 1902, it put on through expresses from Liverpool and Manchester (daily from the latter city) in conjunction with the Great Central Railway. Also, in conjunction with the LNWR, it ran similar services from Birmingham and, later on before World

War I, the West Riding of Yorkshire.

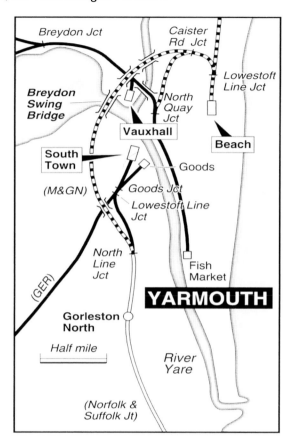

The railways of Great Yarmouth

The Yarmouth herring fishery expanded greatly in the last quarter of the nineteenth century as a result of the involvement of the Scots and the replacement of the sailing drifter by the steam drifter. In 1913, a record year, some 1,000 vessels were fishing from Yarmouth catching and selling herring worth about £1,000,000. In September/October each year special trains had to be laid on from Scotland to bring the Scots fisher girls who carried out the gutting and packing of herrings in the curing yards. This involved shifting some 4,000 workers by rail annually in each direction.

The type of labels used on luggage belonging to Scottish workers travelling by rail to Yarmouth for the autumn herring season

By the early years of the present century, Yarmouth had become the best-served town of its size in the British Isles so far as rail facilities were concerned. The summer non-stop trains between Liverpool Street and Yarmouth were introduced by the Great Eastern in 1904 and continued until the outbreak of war in 1914. The schedule of 150 minutes for the 121.7 miles called for good locomotive work for there were severe speed restrictions through Colchester, Ipswich, Woodbridge and Beccles as well as the need to slow to walking pace for the swing bridges at Beccles and St. Olaves to pick up and set down the pilotman.

The 'Radical Alterations' timetable which came into operation in October 1914 brought about substantial improvements despite the outbreak of war. A fast midday service was put on between Liverpool Street and Yarmouth South Town departing at 12.30pm and reaching Yarmouth at 3.24pm, the corresponding up train leaving South Town at 11.5am and being due in London at 1.55pm. Both of these trains had sections to or from Norwich and Cromer and also Lowestoft, detached or joined at Ipswich and Beccles respectively. This new train, if loaded up to fifteen bogies, was worked by a 4-6-0 '1500' class locomotive or, if loaded up to twelve, by a 'Claud Hamilton' 4-4-0. The exigencies of the war soon had their effect however, resulting in the reduction and deceleration of train services which later in the conflict bore little or no resemblance to those operating at the outbreak.

So far as the Midland & Great Northern (M&GN) was concerned, the daily all-year-round service of through trains from the Midlands and the North had stayed fairly constant throughout the period until 1914. There were two regular daily trains between Birmingham, Leicester and Yarmouth and Lowestoft with through carriages to Norwich and Cromer, one of these trains including through coaches to and from Manchester Central. There can be no doubt that the M&GN was instrumental in popularising the Yarmouth and Cromer areas for holidays with Midlanders and Northerners.

The 150minute non-stop schedules were resumed after the war and continued by the London and North Eastern Railway. Services were then much as they had been in Great Eastern days, timings not improving on pre-1914 performances.

One notable feature, however, was the running of the 'Eastern Belle' (the former 'Clacton Pullman') which, beginning in 1929, on weekdays in summer ran to different resorts in East Anglia on certain days of the week. By 1939, this train was timed to reach Yarmouth (on those days when it served that town) in 2½ hours and Lowestoft in two hours 25 minutes.

The extension of holidays with pay in the inter-war years led to the development of holiday camps both north and south of Yarmouth. Several of these camps were located between Hemsby and Yarmouth in one direction and at Gorleston, Hopton and Corton in the other. A number of halts were opened by the M&GN to serve those north of Yarmouth and, for a time, a steam railcar worked a service to and from the holiday camps. The service continued into British Railways days using a conventional train.

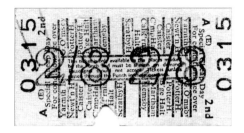

A ticket issued by British Railways in September 1958 for a journey between Yarmouth Beach and Potter Heigham on the "Halt" service.

Some through trains were provided at Easter and on summer Saturdays from Liverpool Street to Caister, reached by reversing at Antingham Road Junction (on the North Walsham - Mundesley branch).

Traffic on the M&GN on summer Saturdays in the 1930s between the Midlands and the North and Yarmouth/Lowestoft was very heavy indeed, as many as 40 trains sometimes running in one direction all of which, in addition to the regular service, had to be fitted in on a system which was 60% single track (the M&GN total mileage was 183 of which 109 was single track).

In contrast to World War I, there was considerable damage to the railway system at Yarmouth during World War II. On 16th February 1941, Gorleston North station was severely damaged during an air raid, so severely in fact, that it was later closed on 5th October 1942. During a raid an 7th May 1943 South Town station was damaged and a bomb, before exploding and in the course of its flight, severed both sets of rails some distance from Vauxhall station, passed through two passenger coaches and exploded on the roadway outside the station which suffered blast damage.

After the establishment of British Railways, traffic to Yarmouth was still heavy for a number of years. On summer Saturdays there were as many as 25 trains in each direction between Liverpool Street and Yarmouth including a holiday camp special for Gorleston routed via Lowestoft. On 5th June 1950 a new named express 'The Easterling' began running, leaving Liverpool Street at 11.03am non-stop to Beccles where it divided, the Yarmouth South Town portion being timed at arrive at 1.42pm and the Lowestoft Central section three minutes later. The return departures were at 7.10pm from both Yarmouth and Lowestoft and at 7.35pm

Class 7MT 4-6-2 No. 70000 *Britannia* at Yarmouth South Town sheds after arriving in the town with "The Easterling". (*PK*)

from Beccles with a 10.00pm arrival at Liverpool Street.

The 1950s proved to be something of an 'Indian Summer' for Britain's railways, for big changes were impending which were to lead to the decline or extinction of many services. The spread of holidays abroad brought about by jet aircraft, the phenomenal growth of travel by private car and the increase in road haulage were all to have far-reaching consequences.

In the Yarmouth area, the first casualty was the Breydon Viaduct. This was in need of major repairs and maintenance costs were also a factor in the decision to close it and divert traffic. It was closed to traffic on 21st September 1953 and this resulted in the withdrawal of through coaches to and from Lowestoft on the Leicester expresses, and the loss of the service between Yarmouth Beach and Lowestoft. However, a service was maintained to Lowestoft from Yarmouth South Town while in the following year during the summer months a through service was started from Derby and Leicester to Lowestoft by way of the former Great Eastern routes.

On the night of 31st January 1953, high tides on the East Coast coinciding with severe gales resulted in the sea rising several feet higher than predicted with disastrous consequences. Inundation of low-lying areas caused damage on a scale unequalled within living memory. At Yarmouth, both South Town and Vauxhall stations were flooded and the line between the latter terminus and Reedham was breached at Berney Arms, while a similar situation developed on the main line at Belton and at Aldeby. Lowestoft station was flooded to a depth of 3ft and the line from there to Reedham and Norwich was breached in several places at Haddiscoe. A major blow came a few years later when it was revealed that almost the entire M&GN system was to close. This was announced in a statement to the press on 13th June 1958, giving reasons for the decision which had been recommended in a report of a special committee set up to examine the situation.

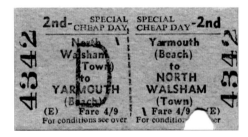

Ticket issued on 28th February 1959.
The last day of services from Yarmouth Beach

It was estimated that the saving would be in the order of £640,000 per annum and a further £500,000 would he required within four years for essential engineering work. The formal enquiry before the East Anglian Transport Users' Consultative Committee was held in the Shire Hall at Norwich on 14th/15th October 1958 and resulted in that body approving closure proposals

which were implemented on 28th February 1959.

Later in the year, on 2nd November, the East Suffolk line from Beccles to Yarmouth South Town was closed to passenger traffic and through services from Liverpool Street and Ipswich were diverted via Lowestoft Central and the Norfolk & Suffolk Joint Line through Gorleston, necessitating the improvement of the track and the strengthening of bridges.

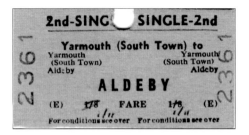

Ticket issued on 1st November 1959.
The last day of services over the Yarmouth South Town-Beccles line.

Between 1958 and 1961 Yarmouth Vauxhall was reconstructed, two of the platforms being lengthened and certain improvements made to assist train operation. New station buildings were provided and extra sidings put in.

On the East Suffolk line, commencing on 5th January 1959, diesel multiple units were introduced on services between Ipswich and Yarmouth South Town and between Ipswich and Lowestoft. The Lowestoft trains called only at Woodbridge, Saxmundham, Halesworth and Beccles, reversing at Lowestoft and continuing to Yarmouth calling intermediately at Gorleston only. The direct trains to Yarmouth called at all stations on the East Suffolk main line.

The line from Westerfield to Lowestoft, and the coast line to Yarmouth South Town appeared in the Beeching proposals for closure in 1963, with rail access to Yarmouth and Lowestoft to be concentrated via Norwich. The situation then was that the basic service was at two-hourly intervals between Ipswich and Yarmouth South Town with additional trains giving an overall hourly service over the Halesworth-Yarmouth section. A number of through trains continued to run between Lowestoft and Liverpool Street. There was, however, persistent speculation that British Railways wished to close the lines as they were unprofitable.

In the event, the line between Westerfield and Lowestoft was spared from closure due largely to the vigorous campaign waged by the East Suffolk Travellers Association. It was designated a 'basic railway', the track was later singled with passing loops, and conductor guards provided. Level crossings were mostly converted to automatic operation. The Liverpool Street-Lowestoft-Gorleston-Yarmouth through trains ceased entirely in 1966, although one buffet car express from Liverpool Street to Lowestoft survived on weekdays and the last through London-Lowestoft working was not withdrawn until 14th May 1984.

The dieselisation of express services on the Great Eastern line began in 1958 and, following the remodelling of the timetable which came into effect on 17th June 1962, the policy was followed of bringing most of the Yarmouth through trains from Liverpool Street to Vauxhall via Norwich (running either into and out of Thorpe or using the Wensum Curve). Overall times between London and Yarmouth via Norwich were 156 minutes down and 155 up. Later on, all these trains were run on this route which was favoured in preference to that via Lowestoft and the coastal line through Gorleston to Yarmouth South Town which had until then seemed likely to become the main line.

The first sign of the impending demise of the latter route came in April 1963 with the publication of the Beeching Report which, as already mentioned, recommended the whole line from Westerfield to Great Yarmouth for closure. However, the former Norfolk & Suffolk Joint line between Yarmouth South Town and Lowestoft Central survived for a further seven years.

In July 1964, freight services were withdrawn from Hopton and Corton followed just over two years later on 12th September 1966 by the designation of these stations, plus Lowestoft North and Gorleston-on-Sea, as unstaffed halts (similar to Gorleston Links Halt which had been opened in July 1914), the diesel units from then onwards having conductor-guards. The withdrawal of freight services from Yarmouth South Town and Lowestoft North was the next step on 6th November 1967 when the line was singled. Finally on 4th May 1970, the railway was closed completely between Lowestoft and Yarmouth together with South Town station, leaving Vauxhall as the only surviving station in the town, and all journeys to and from Yarmouth from that date had to be made via Norwich. The locations where Gorleston-on-Sea, Gorleston North and Yarmouth South Town stations once were are now part of dual carriageway roads.

After the closure of the M&GN, through services between Yarmouth and the Midlands and the North were maintained by way of the former Great Eastern route. These services continued on a considerable scale, the summer 1992 timetable including trains to and from Nottingham, Sheffield, Manchester and Liverpool and also Leicester and Birmingham with a number of additional services starting from or terminating at Norwich, but with Yarmouth connections. For a number of years a reduced service operated in the winter months.

Great Yarmouth was formerly one of the principal herring ports in the world but the industry virtually ceased there in the mid-60s. The servicing of North Sea oil and gas rigs and platforms has since become an important element in the economies of both Yarmouth and Lowestoft. The street tramway serving the fish market and the port closed on 1st January 1976 and all goods facilities at Vauxhall were withdrawn in March 1985 with the result that the railway now plays no part in freight traffic at Yarmouth. A much publicised freight revival in 2000 turned out to be short lived.

On 4th October 1982, the new depot at Crown Point, Norwich, was brought into use, being opened formally by Sir Peter Parker (then Chairman of British Rail) on 27th October. The new depot was provided for the servicing, examination and maintenance of Norwich allocated locomotive hauled stock, diesel multiple units and diesel shunting locomotives. It could also provide servicing and some repairs to main line locomotives operating the London and cross-country services. The depot was a £10 million investment and initially employed nearly 200 staff. Rolling stock servicing at Yarmouth (and also Lowestoft) ceased, and was transferred to the new depot. Also on 4th October 1982, through trains between London and Great Yarmouth were reduced to one each way (the re-instated 'East Anglian'). This train left Yarmouth at 07.15am, stopping only at Norwich and Ipswich. The return working left London Liverpool Street at 4.20pm.

Early in 1984, it was announced that closure notices were to be posted for the Reedham - Yarmouth line at the end of the year. In February of that year, the East Norfolk Travellers' Association called a protest meeting, and in September of the following year, British Rail informed local councils that it would require an annual subsidy of £52,500 if it was to continue running the service, this being 50% of the sum required to cover maintenance and track renewals over the next five years. It stated that if half of the £105,000 required every year were raised by outside bodies it was prepared to find the rest.

Great Yarmouth Council, fearing that the Acle direct line would he unable to handle the additional summer Saturday traffic from the Midlands and the North, announced that it was willing to make a contribution as were Yarmouth Port & Haven Commissioners and other local users groups. Norfolk County Council then voted very narrowly (38-37) to make up the balance whereupon British Rail announced that closure plans for the line had been dropped.

Over thirty years after the closure of Breydon Viaduct, a new bridge was opened over Breydon Water on 24th May 1986 to carry the Great Yarmouth by-pass. This road used the former M&GN railway formation from near the site of the Yarmouth South Town station, over Breydon Water and across the present tracks leading to Yarmouth Vauxhall station. The site of Yarmouth South Town had been cleared in the late 1970s.

On 11th May 1987, electrification of the main line from London to Norwich was completed and the journey time between London and Yarmouth reduced to just over 2½ hours in either direction (by 'The East Anglian' 2 hour 13 minutes down and 2 hours 28 minutes up). There were twelve services down and fourteen up during weekdays and nine each way on Sundays, all involving changing trains at Norwich for Great Yarmouth.

In the 1990s, British Rail ran a limited number of through trains between London and Great Yarmouth in both directions on summer Saturdays. *The Railway Magazine* for May 1992 reported "The three return Saturday Holidaymaker services between London and Great Yarmouth continue to be popular and due to demand will run for a longer period than last year from early July to the end of September". Evidence, if such were needed, that Yarmouth was retaining its appeal as a popular holiday resort despite the great changes which have taken place in the last fifty years or so.

This article, which was updated with minor amendments in 2005, first appeared in **Back Track,** *considered Britain's Leading Historical Monthly railway magazine in 1992.*
It has been reproduced here by kind permission of Mrs. June Frost and the editor of **Back Track** *magazine, Mr. Michael Blakemore.*

REVIEW OF RAIL SERVICES AND FACILITIES IN THE LATE 20TH AND EARLY 21ST CENTURY

Great Yarmouth once had a considerable railway presence but since 1970 has relied upon what was previously know as Vauxhall station as the entry point to the town for all rail travellers. At one time the area had three main and several small stations such as Newtown Halt, Caister and those at Gorleston. The position of the remaining station has been described as "being at the back of the town" and can be quite difficult to access in the summer traffic jams which are common on the road network surrounding the station. Both South Town and Beach stations, now distant memories for those who used them, were better placed for the town centre with station access influenced to a lesser extent by road traffic entering and leaving the town.

Within the town there was extensive railway access to many of the industrial areas from the main stations, but like so much of the past railway network at Great Yarmouth these have been totally erased from the landscape. From South Town, two tracks crossed the road outside the station to gain access to a goods shed, riverside coal yards, a wood importers yard and other businesses. At least twelve wagon turntables were in use in 1905 to achieve the required flexibility in the restricted areas. Little evidence remains today of the important tramway goods line that served the existing port and quayside premises until the end of 1975. This line carried vast amounts of goods to and from Yarmouth Vauxhall and Beach stations to the port and the fishwharf, and gave full rail access to the once important Lacons brewery premises. The tramway carried thousands of tons of fish, grain, wood, coal, salt and other materials for riverside firms and business such as Wenn's, Steward & Patterson, Trinity House, Birds Eye and A. King. Indeed many private sidings were served by this tramway.

At the time of writing (2005), the Government has announced support for the proposal to build a new harbour and ferry terminal at Great Yarmouth. Details released of the new harbour show access would be by road only. The now recovered quayside tramway goods line at one time ventured as far as the Lower Ferry and not far from the planned location of the new harbour. The pattern of rail services in the mid 1990s and at the start of the 21st century varied considerably both for cross country and London services. The decline in through services to Great Yarmouth is noticeable. The timetable for the peak cross country summer Saturday services in 1995 when operated by Regional Railways, provided travellers with six through services to Liverpool. However, for the same period in 1998, with the operator changed to Central Trains, only two trains to Peterborough and two to Liverpool were shown. By 1999, a further reduction is seen and for 2004, no through cross-country services were provided.

It was with much publicity in 1999, that Anglia Railways announced new daily services to London from Yarmouth. These would commence on 27th September and use the latest Class 170 Turbostar units with trains leaving Yarmouth for London at 0715hrs and 1824hrs.

The franchise to run the rail services in the majority of East Anglia passed from Anglia Railways to the National Express Group plc operator "one" in April 2004. The London through services timetable, prepared by "one" and which commenced on 12th December 2004, did not show Great Yarmouth on the network map despite the town having one weekday through service to the capital which left Yarmouth station at 0622hrs, with the return train leaving Liverpool Street at 1700hrs. In the same timetable, neighbouring Lowestoft had six weekday direct services to London via the East Suffolk line, with eight on Saturdays.

Until late 1959, Yarmouth South Town station and the East Suffolk Line provided the town with a fast and direct route to the capital. Since 1999, after a lapse of many years, the East Suffolk line has seen frequent London through services which in addition to serving Lowestoft and Oulton Broad, provide good communication links to important small towns such as Beccles, Halesworth, Saxmundham and Woodbridge. The site of South Town station for so long the main station for London, is now a dual carriage road, as is much of the track bed from that station. Many newcomers to the area may not initially realise that South Town and Beach stations ever existed, or be aware of the substantial loss of rail travel opportunities the town has suffered with the major railway closures that have been inflicted upon it.

Right - A photograph of a poster on display at Yarmouth Beach station in early 1959.

BRITISH RAILWAYS

WITHDRAWAL OF SERVICES
MELTON CONSTABLE TO YARMOUTH (BEACH)

The British Transport Commission hereby give notice that on and from 2nd March 1959 the passenger and freight train services will be withdrawn from the undermentioned stations :

Aylsham (North)	Felmingham	North Walsham (Town)
Caister-on-Sea	Great Ormesby	Potter Heigham
Caister Camp Halt	Hemsby	Potter Heigham Bridge Halt
California Halt	Honing	Scratby Halt
Catfield	Martham	Stalham
Corpusty & Saxthorpe	Newtown Halt	Yarmouth (Beach)

Passengers will be catered for by the following omnibus undertakings operating in the area :

Eastern Counties Omnibus Company
Seagull Coaches Ltd.

Details of the Eastern Counties Omnibus Company's alternative road services are shown on a separate notice and details of Seagull Coaches services can be obtained from their timetables

Freight and parcels collection and delivery services will continue to be operated in the areas at present served from the above stations

Facilities for all full wagon load freight traffic will be available as follows
Aylsham (North) at Aylsham (South)
Catfield at North Walsham (Main) or Wroxham
Corpusty & Saxthorpe at Aylsham (South) or Melton Constable
Felmingham at North Walsham (Main)
Honing at North Walsham (Main) or Worstead
North Walsham (Town) at North Walsham (Main)
Potter Heigham at North Walsham (Main) or Acle
Stalham at North Walsham (Main) or Wroxham
Caister-on-Sea at Yarmouth (Vauxhall)
Great Ormesby at Yarmouth (Vauxhall)
Hemsby at Yarmouth (Vauxhall)
Martham at Yarmouth (Vauxhall) or Acle
Yarmouth (Beach) at Yarmouth (Vauxhall)

Further information can be obtained from Mr. G. G. Goodings, Traffic Manager, British Railways, Eastern Region, Norwich, or the local station master

YARMOUTH BEACH

In November 1883, the Eastern & Midlands Railway purchased from the London & North Western Railway a pair of 2-4-0 mixed traffic locomotives. One of these, No. 43A, is seen here at Yarmouth Beach. Built in 1857 for the Lancaster and Carlisle Railway by Rothwell, Hick & Rothwell at the Union Foundry in Bolton, No. 43A was broken up at Melton Constable in 1905. (*CTC*)

An example of the unique atmosphere that surrounded Yarmouth Beach is sampled here as M&GNJR Class A 4-4-0 No. 30 leaves with a train for the Norfolk & Suffolk Joint line stations and Lowestoft. It appears that the tender of this particular engine gave protection to the crew when running tender first. No. 30 was built by Beyer Peacock & Co. in 1886 and withdrawn from service in 1933. (*StationsUK*)

Headed by M&GNJR Class A 4-4-2T No. 41, a train from Lowestoft arrives at Beach station in the mid 1920s. In the 1930s, all three locomotives of this class had their side tanks raked which enhanced their appearance as well as improving visibility for the footplate crew. Of interest is the number of six wheeled coaches included in the train. (*HC*)

Another of the Class A 4-4-2T locomotives over the pit at Beach shed. When built these tank locomotives were intended for use on services over both N&SJRC lines. No. 20, seen here complete with raised brass numbers, was built in 1909.(*RAS*)

The M&GNJR inherited from the Eastern & Midlands Railway the elegant Class A 4-4-0s, of which No. 26 was one. Built by Beyer Peacock & Co. at Manchester in 1883, No. 26 was taken out of service in November 1936. It is seen here at Beach station in the early years of its life. (MWC)

The wide expanse of the main platform at Yarmouth Beach shows up well in this 1913 print of Class C 4-4-0 No. 1 about to leave with a train for the M&GNJR line. In the background a Class A 4-4-0 locomotive can be seen. No. 1 was designed by S. W. Johnson and built in 1894 by Sharp, Stewart. It was withdrawn from service in November 1937. (CTC)

Another of the versatile M&GNJR Class C 4-4-0s, No. 12, prepares to leave Beach yard with a goods train. This locomotive gained the flower pot type chimney in the mid 1930s and was withdrawn from service in August 1942.
(Photo Courtesy RCTS/DWA0091)

The main buildings of Yarmouth Beach station as seen from Nelson Road North in the 1950s. The passenger entrance was up the steps in the gap between the white painted buildings or further along in the opening between the white painted and plain brick building. Another entrance and favoured by most local passengers, was through the large gates which opened onto Nelson Road North and which were immediately south of the main buildings. *(MWC)*

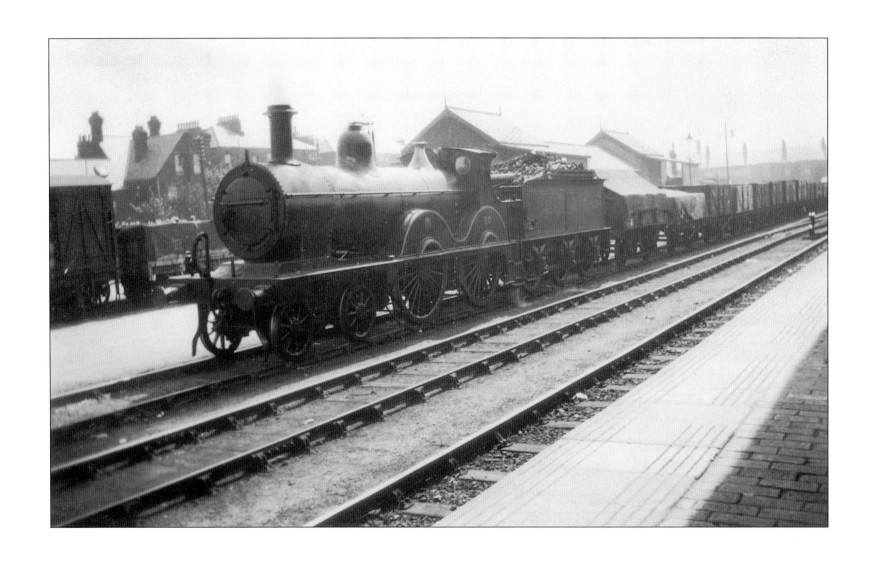

A goods train waits to leave Beach station in August 1925 headed by M&GNJR Class C 4-4-0 No. 80. Behind the train is the goods shed, a prominent feature of Beach station. Built by Beyer, Peacock in 1899, No. 80 was withdrawn from service in February 1937. *(MWC)*

A view looking north along the main platform and under the canopy at Yarmouth Beach. Passengers using the slope on the centre left would be able to leave the station by the gates mentioned on page 21. (CTC)

For many years the M&GNJR carried hundreds of workers from Scotland to Great Yarmouth for them to participate in the autumn herring fishing. The great majority of these workers were ladies, known locally as the "Scotch girls", who carried out the gutting, cleaning and packing of the herring which had been caught by the large fleet of English and Scottish herring drifters. A group of these ladies are seen here about to join the Yarmouth Beach to Aberdeen train in the 1920s. (MWC)

The main entrance to the goods depot was in Euston Road. A military parade marches past the entrance in M&GNJR days. (CTC)

Withdrawn in February 1937, M&GNJR Class C 4-4-0 No. 80, is seen here the previous year on shed at Yarmouth Beach. No. 80 was built by Beyer, Peacock in 1899. (Photo Courtesy RCTS/WHI0116)

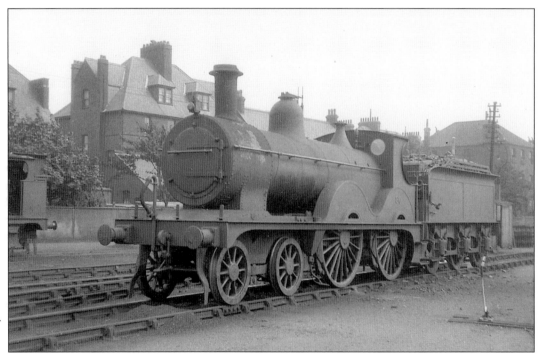

A fine view of M&GNJR Class D 0-6-0 No. 68, which has just arrived with a goods train at Yarmouth Beach station. Designed by S.W. Johnson and built by Kitson & Co. in 1899, No. 68 was withdrawn from service in 1937.(*MWC*)

One of the three M&GNJR Class A 4-4-2T locomotives, No. 41, waits to leave Beach station with a passenger train in 1925. Completed in December 1904 at Melton Constable, No. 41 was withdrawn from service as LNER No. 041 in January 1944. (*MWC*)

Shortly after the take-over of the M&GNJR by the LNER in 1936, a former M&GNJR Class C 4-4-0 arrives at Yarmouth Beach with a goods train as LNER No. 06. Built in 1894 by Sharp, Stewart to a design by S.W. Johnson, No. 6 was withdrawn in March 1944. (*MWC*)

With the demise of the M&GNJR and the LNER in control, the scene changed and locomotives from the LNER replaced the M&GN types.
The GNR Class C12 4-4-2 locomotives were built for suburban work but later found to be well suited to East Anglian branch line work. Soon members of the class were allocated to East Anglian sheds. LNER No. 4015 is seen at Beach station in 1937. The corrugated iron roofed engine shed can be seen in the background. (*Photo Courtesy RCTS/DWA0231*)

The Class D2 4-4-0 was another GNR locomotive type to be seen at Beach. No. 4327 of that class is seen there in early 1938. The Class D2 locomotives were introduced in 1897.
(*Photo Courtesy RCTS/DWA0247*)

Moving on to the 1950s and we find Class D16/3 4-4-0 No. 62517 waiting to leave Beach station with a stopping train for the former M&GNJR line. No. 62517 was a well known Yarmouth engine in the 1950s having spent periods allocated to South Town (32D), Vauxhall (32E) and Beach (32F) during those years. (*MWC*)

A view looking north from the main platform at Yarmouth Beach during the summer of 1957. Ivatt 4MT 2-6-0 No. 43148 can be seen on the right, standing outside the engine shed and on the approach to the turntable. (CTC)

The view from the very end of the platform with a Class B12/3 4-6-0 backing down to the station. (CTC)

In this view recorded during the summer of 1958, a Class D16/3 4-4-0 locomotive waits to leave Beach station with a stopping train. (*CTC*)

Many believe that diesel motive power was never seen at Yarmouth Beach. In addition to being used in connection with the track removal and general clearance of the station area after closure, diesel shunters had been working at Yarmouth Beach for a number of years. Introduced in 1955, the Hunslet Class 05 0-6-0 locomotives had a Gardner 8L3 engine developing 204hp at 1200rpm.
One of the class, No. 11174, is seen here working in the yard on shunting duties. (*CTC*)

Another summer scene from 1958 at Beach station and the last summer ever for the former M&GNJR at Yarmouth. During that year there were three Class B12/3 4-6-0 locomotives allocated to Beach, one of which is seen waiting to leave with a passenger train. Despite the permanence of this scene, within twelve months it would be gone. (CTC)

Recorded on the same day as the previous photograph but looking towards the station building and goods shed. The future use for Beach station and the yard was to be a car park and coach station. However, it seems that in 1958 it was already being used by coaches since six can be seen here, at least four of which appear to be products of the Eastern Coach Works at nearby Lowestoft. (CTC)

A view of the engine shed at Beach station a few days before closure. (*MWC*)

It is the 28th February 1959, and the last day of rail services from Yarmouth to the Midlands via the former M&GNJR. Ivatt 4MT 2-6-0 No. 43160 is seen at the coaling plant prior to working one of the remaining services from Beach station. This locomotive was allocated to Beach shed for many years. (*CTC*)

YARMOUTH BEACH 1959 (*All MW*)
Top Left 1st March - Looking north from Sandown Road. **Centre Left** 21st June - Looking north from Sandown Road. **Bottom Left** 21st June - The track bed to Lowestoft and the Yarmouth Union Railway. **Top Right** 1st March - Looking south from Sandown Road. **Centre Right** 30th April - Looking south from Sandown Road. **Bottom Right** 21st June - Looking south from Sandown Road.

After the closure of Yarmouth Beach and the majority of the former M&GNJR, the removal of the track and signalling at Yarmouth and other strategic locations was quickly carried out. With all the track having been removed in the immediate station area, the demolition train is seen here working north of the level crossing near Yarmouth Yard signal box. After the closure, Beach station and the former yard and engine shed site became a coach station. (*Archant*)

YARMOUTH SOUTH TOWN

The well-known front of Yarmouth South Town station in the 1950s. Unfortunately the usually reliable station clock was under repair at the time this image was recorded. *(PTP)*

Another view of the station front looking somewhat like a stately home. This scene is thought to have been recorded in the 1870s. *(CTC)*

A fine view of the High Mill which was situated between Mill Road and High Mill Road could be achieved from the station forecourt. With the station on the left, the mill, which was built in 1812 and demolished in 1905, dominated the railway at South Town. It was claimed to be the tallest mill ever built in Europe being 122 feet high. (*CTC*)

Turning to the left the photographer would look down the side of the station and see the railway lines that crossed South Town Road to gain access to goods sheds, coal and wood merchants yards, a mill and other riverside properties. (*PTP*)

A fine selection of advertising signs decorate the walls of a clean and tidy Yarmouth South Town in this view of the concourse from the early 1940s. (PTP)

As with all busy stations the environment is not always as smart and clean as one would like. Following World War 11, South Town in the late 1940s still looked a little run down, but this was soon remedied after overdue maintenance and renewal work had been carried out. (MWC)

A fine study of LNER B17/2 4-6-0 No. 2813 *Woodbastwick Hall* on the South Town turntable in October 1932. Entering service in 1930, *Woodbastwick Hall* was renumbered No. 61613 in August 1949 and rebuilt as a Class B17/6 locomotive during December 1951. Withdrawal from traffic at Cambridge shed came in December 1959, with scrapping at Doncaster being carried out the following month. *(RAS)*

Although this scene is from 1911, the infrastructure remained essentially unaltered until the end of steam hauled services from South Town in 1960. With a GER Class Y14 0-6-0 (later to become LNER Class J15) locomotive standing near a water crane and the ash disposal area, the engine shed, together with the top of the shearlegs can be seen. These shearlegs were a prominent feature of Yarmouth South Town shed. The vast area of open countryside and railway land seen on this print has now been developed into retail, business and industrial estates, and roads. *(HMRS/ H. F. Hilton Coll'n)*

An everyday scene at Yarmouth South Town from the 1950s that will bring back memories to those who travelled from the station. In Platform 2 the stock of a London train can be seen, and on the concourse, the W. H. Smith bookstall. Whilst all trace of this important station has been erased from the landscape, one of the seats seen here near the bookstall was saved, and is now an exhibit at the National Railway Museum at York. *(StationsUK)*

During January 1953 parts of the railway network in Norfolk and Suffolk were seriously affected by flooding with many instances of track being damaged or undermined. Both Vauxhall and South Town were among the stations flooded as well as the rail lines to those stations. With the water receded and the track passed for running with restrictions, the first London service over the Yarmouth South Town- Beccles line slowly leaves South Town headed by Class B17/6 4-6-0 No. 61665 *Leicester City*. Allocated to Yarmouth South Town for many years, *Leicester City* was withdrawn from that shed in April 1959 and cut up at Doncaster in June 1959. The bridge that the train is passing under was another of those over which trains between Yarmouth Beach and Lowestoft passed. Closed in 1953 it was south of the Breydon Bridge and north of Gorleston North junction. This location is now a major traffic interchange and roundabout with newcomers to the area having no idea that the railway was ever there, all signs of it having been erased by major development projects which include four new roads, together with Tesco and B&Q superstores and other commercial and industrial premises. (*Archant*)

Having just arrived at South Town with a train from London Liverpool Street, Class B17/6 4-6-0 No. 61622 *Alnwick Castle* rests at the buffers. The loss of fast direct through services from Great Yarmouth to the capital was a major blow and despite reassurances that good alternatives would be provided from Vauxhall, the direct route is still badly missed with the great majority of passengers travelling between Great Yarmouth and London having to change trains at Norwich. No. 61622 was completed in 1931 and withdrawn from service at South Town in September 1958. *(CTC)*

One of the few remaining inside cylinder Class B12/3 4-6-0s, No. 61572 arrives at Yarmouth South Town on 30th July 1958 with a local stopping train. The last two locomotives of this class to be scrapped were Nos. 61535 and 61571, both being cut up at Stratford in January 1960. Now very much a celebrity engine, No. 61572 was withdrawn from British Railways service in September 1961, but remained stored long enough for the engine to be purchased for preservation by the M&GNRPS for use on the North Norfolk Railway. *(MWC)*

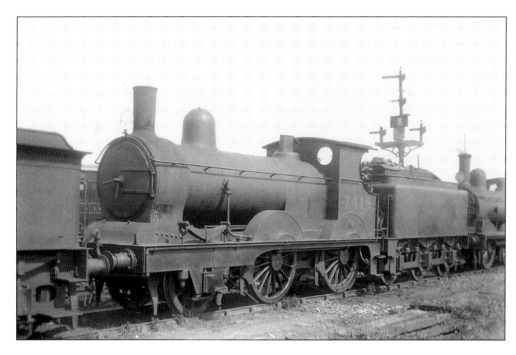

The Class E4 2-4-0s were designed by J. Holden for the GER, and entered service as the Class T26. Members of the class could be found at work right across East Anglia on passenger duties. In the later years of their lives they were employed on light work on branch lines. One example was saved for the National Railway Museum collection and at the time of writing was on loan to the Bressingham Steam Museum near Diss. LNER E4 2-4-0 No. 7415 is seen here on shed at Yarmouth South Town in the early1930s. Built in 1902, this E4 was withdrawn from service in 1937. It is shown here with a dual tender, built in GER days to carry coal or oil. *(Photo Courtesy RCTS/RPP0211)*

In the 1950s, South Town was home to two push-pull fitted Class F5 2-4-2T locomotives which were used extensively on services to Beccles and Lowestoft. Designed by S. D. Holden and introduced in 1911, the F5 was a rebuild of GER Class M15 locomotives (LNER F4). One of the two, No. 67218, is seen leaving Yarmouth South Town on 31st August 1951. *(HC)*

The former GER "Claud Hamilton" 4-4-0s became a common sight at all Great Yarmouth stations. Class D16/2 No. 62553 is seen here at Yarmouth South Town shed, to which it was allocated for three separate periods, one in 1947 and two in 1949. Other sheds to which this engine was allocated were Norwich and Ipswich. During 1949, No. 62553 was rebuilt and emerged from the works as a Class D16/3. Completed at Stratford in November 1906 as GER No. 1842, No. 62553 was scrapped in January 1957. (*MWC*)

The Class J15 0-6-0 locomotives were a versatile design equally at home on goods or passenger duties. Designed by T. W. Worsdell for the GER and introduced in 1883, they could be found throughout East Anglia and outlasted many later types of steam locomotives. Some of the class were still working almost to the end of East Anglian steam. On 9th July 1950, class member No. 65390 was to be found at Yarmouth South Town shed in the company of two Class D16/3 4-4-0s and in front of the large modern Yarmouth South Town signal box. A survivor of the class, No. 65462, was saved from scrapping by the M&GNRPS and can usually be found at home on the North Norfolk Railway. (SLS)

Class B17/4 4-6-0 No. 61664 *Liverpool* was frequently seen at Yarmouth South Town and on 30th July 1958 was preparing to depart with a train to London Liverpool Street. A Derby lightweight dmu is arriving on Platform 3 and insulated containers can be seen on the left, these being used for the dispatch of Birds Eye frozen products from the factory in the town. *Liverpool* was withdrawn from March shed in June 1960 and immediately scrapped at Stratford. (FC)

Although steam traction continued to the end, haulage of South Town's direct London services became more dependant on diesel locomotives as the closure date in 1959 approached. Having worked in direct from London Liverpool Street, two Brush Type 2 locomotives are seen here on shed at Yarmouth South Town. (PK)

In the latter days of steam traction, the numerous former GER 2-4-2T and GNR 4-4-2T steam locomotives were superseded on local services from South Town by Class N7 0-6-2T locomotives. Class member No. 69690, had only just been reallocated from Cambridge when the scene was recorded in July 1958 and is seen here in company with a Metropolitan Cammell dmu. These and similar types of units were well established by 1958 on many local services, as the days of steam operation were drawing to a close. (FC)

South Town station finally closed in 1970 with the closure of the Lowestoft line, although many prefer to think of the closure from when the London services were withdrawn. With no London services, the remains of the station still used for railway purposes rapidly became a very depressing and untidy sight.

A Lowestoft service formed of the hybrid unit extensively used on the line in the last few weeks, departs from Yarmouth South Town. (CTC)

After the closure of the Beccles line, the London through services ran for a few years via Gorleston and Lowestoft. However by the end of 1966, these had all been diverted to Yarmouth Vauxhall. With goods facilities already closed, the only requirement at South Town was for a single track to Lowestoft. All other track was removed and here we see Brush Class 31/1 A1A-A1A locomotive No. D5523 with a track recovery train and steam crane at South Town. A few signals remained in operation, but these were all recovered as the demolition progressed. D5523 was later renumbered 31105. (PK)

Platform Four was the only one still with track in the last years of Yarmouth South Town. Here the platform accommodates the hybrid unit that is waiting to return to Lowestoft. (*CTC*)

The derelict platforms two and three at South Town with the hybrid unit in Platform Four. At that time the main station building was in use by a company involved in the offshore oil and gas industry. (*CTC*)

Researching Great Yarmouth's railway heritage is helped by having many images of the early railway scene in the town available, such as these prints featuring South Town in the 1870s, two of which feature 2-4-0 No. 73. *(MWC and CTC)*

YARMOUTH VAUXHALL

Vauxhall has undergone a number of major changes since the station was established. Significant changes were made in the late 1950s and early 1960s when it was extensively modernised and partly enlarged, and in the in the early 1980s, when changes were made to the overall roof. The exterior of Vauxhall in the mid 1950s is captured in this view. *(Archant)*

Complete with one of the Corporation electric tramcars standing outside the station, this view is from the period immediately before the First World War. The 3' 6" gauge electric tramway opened in Great Yarmouth on 19th June 1902 with further routes opening in 1905 and 1907. It ceased running to Vauxhall in 1928 and had gained access to the station by crossing the bridge over the Bure near to the station. The bridge was shared with the railway tramway which ran from Vauxhall to the quayside and Fishwharf. (*CTC*)

The exterior of the station building in 2005 when known as "Great Yarmouth Station", and operated by the Train Operating Company, 'one' Railway. (*MW*)

A scene from LNER days showing the interior of the station and a wonderful selection of advertisements on the walls. (*CTC*)

Several types of locomotives were used on the tramway through the town including LNER Class J65 0-6-0T No. 7158 which ran on the quayside lines with the front coupling rods removed. The engine is seen here in the yard at Yarmouth Vauxhall after a trip to the Fishwharf. Much has been written concerning the requirement to enclose the motion of engines used on the tramway, but obviously this rule was subject to variation. Built as GER Class E22 0-6-0T No. 158 at Stratford in 1899, No. 7158 was scrapped in 1932. The GER built 20 of these J. Holden designed light branch locomotives between 1889 and 1893, one of which was allocated to Yarmouth Beach for many years. (*MWC*)

G.E.R. PLATFORMS, VAUXHALL STATION.

The splendour of the Great Eastern Railway is sampled in this superb scene at Vauxhall from 1904 showing 1892 built Class T26 2-4-0 No. 447 waiting to depart. Despite many alterations to the main building, the layout in 2005 is basically the same as seen here over one hundred years ago. (*CTC*)

A good view of the types of rolling stock in use in 1924 can be obtained from this scene showing a Yarmouth Vauxhall - Norwich train waiting to depart. (*StationsUK*)

The Thompson designed Class L1 2-6-4T locomotives became a familiar sight in East Suffolk and Norfolk during the 1950s, with examples allocated to sheds such as Ipswich, Norwich and Lowestoft. In 1955, Ipswich was home to eleven of these powerful locomotives, of which 100 were built in the years following World War II. One of the class, No. 67736, is seen here at Yarmouth Vauxhall on 18th May 1958. The embankment carrying the former M&GNJR line from Yarmouth Beach to Gorleston North Junction, which closed in 1953, can be seen on the right. (*RAS*)

In the 21st century, a large ASDA superstore and car park occupies the site of Yarmouth Vauxhall shed(32E), turntable and yard. When this scene was recorded on 26th May 1956, supermarkets were unheard of and the shed was host to two Class D16/3 4-4-0s, No. 62517 with modified footplating and, on the turntable, No. 62613 retaining the original footplating.

As mentioned elsewhere, the Class D16/3 locomotives were the result of a succession of rebuilding programmes. Unfortunately, all locomotives of this type were broken up, with No. 62613 being the last in service, withdrawal from traffic coming in 1960. (MWC)

Looking towards the station in 1949 from the former M&GNJR overbridge which carried the line from Yarmouth Beach to Gorleston North Junction, and thereby, gave access to the Lowestoft line from Beach station. The signal box is on the left and the carriage and goods yard are on the right. At the bottom right a Class D16/3 4-4-0 is standing at the coaling stage and water crane. The engine shed would have been on the far right and is seen in the previous print. (StationsUK)

The interior of the station in the mid 1950s with a Derby Lightweight diesel multiple unit in Platform 3, showing the overall roof extending over the platforms. This was later removed leaving only the concourse with a roof. (*StationsUK*)

With the replacement of steam locomotives by diesel electric motive power, the Brush Type 2 A1A-A1A locomotive soon became a familiar sight at Vauxhall especially on summer Saturdays, when Vauxhall was the destination for many through trains from London, the Midlands and the North. Two of the type, on the left No. 31117 and on the right No. 31271, are seen here at Vauxhall. No. 31271 is waiting to depart with a London train, while No. 31177 is waiting to clear Platform 2 after arriving earlier with another through service. (*RF*)

For several years many of the through trains from the Midlands were hauled by Class 25 Bo-Bo diesel electric locomotives. Built by British Railways and powered by a 1250bhp Sulzer 6-cyl 6LDA 28-B engine, the class entered service in 1961. Usually these locomotives worked in pairs on the long haul Yarmouth seaside holidaymaker trains. A frequent sight right across East Anglia at locations such as Acle, Brundall, Norwich, Thetford, March and Peterborough whilst working these trains. One of this popular class is preserved on the North Norfolk Railway. Their train having been removed to the sidings by the resident Class 03, Nos. 25134 and 25278 wait to leave Platform 2 at Vauxhall. (*RF*)

A Brush Class 47/4 Co-Co locomotive leaves Yarmouth Vauxhall with a train for the Midlands in the summer of 1982. In the distance is a Class 37 locomotive and the carriage sidings containing at least three sets of coaches. The Class 47 locomotives, built during 1963-67 by Brush at Loughborough, are powered by a Sulzer 12LDA28C engine. The main generator and traction motors are of Brush manufacture. Many Class 47s remain active in the 21st century with a variety of operators. Independent of high voltage overhead wiring systems and the various problems these have including vandalism, these locomotives are ideal for an assortment of duties including, when required, front line passenger services. (*GM*)

A typical Summer Saturday scene in the early 1980s at Vauxhall with one of many hauled trains to depart from the station leaving behind Brush Class 31/4 AlA AlA No. 31417. The Class 31/4 locomotives were powered by an English Electric 12cylinder 12SV engine developing 1470bhp and had a maximum speed of 90 mph. This particular locomotive entered service as D5856. (*GM*)

Other holiday trains to the coast were powered by Class 37 locomotives, of which No. 37054 is an example. This English Electric Type 3 Co-Co originally carried the number D6754 and is seen clearing the platform after the train that it arrived with, had been removed by the resident Class 03 0-6-0 diesel shunter. (*GM*)

With the need to provide heating facilities in the winter for coaching stock a few surplus Brush Type 2 locomotives were converted into mobile heating units. Painted in dark green livery, these units stood out at a time when locomotives were painted in the corporate blue livery. Departmental carriage heating unit ADB968013 spent long periods at Vauxhall and is seen here in the large yard.

Previously this unit was Class 31/1 A1A A1A No. 31013 and prior to that D5513. (*GM*)

Another hauled train arrives at Vauxhall in the late 1970s hauled by a Class 47/4 Co-Co locomotive. (*GM*)

The carriage maintenance facilities and sidings were quite extensive at Vauxhall. On 28th June 1986, Stratford's Network South East liveried Class 47/4 Co-Co No. 47573 *The Evening Standard* is making use of the sidings together with the stock of the train it arrived with earlier.

Servicing of coaching stock at Yarmouth was withdrawn with the opening of Crown Point Depot at Norwich in October 1982. (*NF*)

Fresh from the paint shop, Main Line liveried Class 31/4 A1A A1A No. 31407 was a surprise visitor to Yarmouth on 7th September 1996. The locomotive is seen here with the stock of a Yarmouth - Liverpool Street through service which it would haul as far as Norwich.

No. 31407 went on to become part of the Fragonset Railways fleet. (*NF*)

A trial resumption of freight services from Yarmouth occurred in 2000 but turned out to be short lived. On 16th March 2000, EWS Class 37/7 Co-Co No. 37895 was at Yarmouth to work a freight out of the town. This locomotive was one of the Class 37s that were refurbished and had the main generator replaced with a Brush BA1005A alternator, regeared bogies fitted and ballast weights added with subsequent greater tractive effort. It was not however subjected to the Mirrless engine upgrade. (*NF*)

A number of derailments have occurred at Vauxhall in the last fifty years. These include a collision between Class D16/3 4-4-0s Nos. 62523 and 62524 on 10th August 1956, a serious collision with coaches being forced off the track and rolling over on 29th July 1961 and minor incidents such as this on 25th August 2001 with a bogie derailed. The Class 47/7 Co-Co locomotive on the train was Rail Express System liveried No. 47787 *Victim Support.* (*NF*)

YARMOUTH - LOWESTOFT- BECCLES

In order to gain access from Beach station to the railway to Lowestoft, several bridges, were constructed. Some crossed rivers, others crossed roads and two spanned railways. This bridge crossed the River Bure in the vicinity of the yacht station. (CTC)

Further south, and after crossing a road bridge and the bridge over the railway lines at Yarmouth Vauxhall station, the railway crossed Breydon Viaduct. By far the best known of all aspects of civil engineering on the M&GNJR, this impressive bridge consisted of five spans, one of which could be swung open to allow the passage of shipping. Closed to rail traffic in 1953, it was demolished in 1962. (MWC)

Serving a vast residential area, a holiday camp and many guest houses and hotels, the station at Gorleston-on-Sea was important and well used. A feature of this station was the large number of mums who used the trains to go shopping in Yarmouth with their children in prams in the guards section of the trains! With through trains to the Midlands and the North and in later years a daily service to London, the station provided the community with a wide selection of travel opportunities. The station area is now a roundabout on the Gorleston bypass and the track bed to Great Yarmouth is a dual carriageway. One of the Yarmouth South Town allocated push-pull fitted Class F5 2-4-2Ts, No. 67218, leaves for Lowestoft propelling the train. (*StationsUK*)

The Class J19 0-6-0s, designed by S. Holden for the GER and introduced in 1912, were rebuilt from 1934 with round topped boilers. One of the class, No. 64643, is seen here in 1959 at Gorleston whilst heading for Lowestoft with empty coaching stock. (*PK*)

Moving on to the diesel era on the coast line and looking down from the station footbridge we find a Derby lightweight diesel multiple unit leaving Gorleston-on-Sea for Yarmouth South Town. (*CTC*)

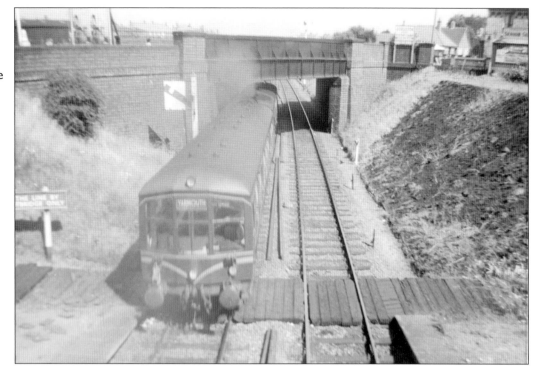

An almost new English Electric Class 37 Co-Co diesel electric locomotive heads a Yarmouth South Town - Liverpool Street express through Gorleston on the former N&SJRC line in 1961. For through trains only stopping at Gorleston-on-Sea station, twenty six minutes was allowed for the journey from Yarmouth to Lowestoft. Many trains included a buffet car and on Saturdays a few stopped at Corton and Hopton. A flood of complaints from residents living in properties along the coast line about noise and vibration from the large number of hauled through trains was a contributory factor in rerouting all the London services to Yarmouth Vauxhall. With the closure of the railway this location became a dual carriageway. One of the popular Class 37s is now preserved at the North Norfolk Railway. (*PK*)

With regular services to London Liverpool Street, both steam and diesel main line locomotives became a common sight at Gorleston in the late 1950s and 1960s. A Class 24 Bo-Bo diesel electric locomotive leaves Gorleston-on-Sea for South Town with a through service from London. The Class 24 locomotives were introduced in 1958 and became a familiar sight working passenger and freight services in East Suffolk. They were powered by a Sulzer 6cyl 6LDA28 engine driving four BTH traction motors. (*CTC*)

A much different scene from the 1960s and a very unusual Yarmouth train. With the Yarmouth South Town - Lowestoft line reduced to a basic single line railway, this very rare image taken from a colour slide shows the weed killing train at work on the line in 1967 hauled by a Brush Class 31 AIA AIA locomotive. (*PK*)

With many holiday camps nearby, the station at Hopton-on-Sea was very busy in the summer. Centrally situated in the village it was one of several stations to have Camping Coaches stabled in a siding. One of these, which provided holiday accommodation on the railway, is on the far right. The twin towers of RAF Hopton can be seen to the left of the church tower. A Class C12 4-4-2T locomotive hauled Lowestoft - Yarmouth train pauses at the station in this 1953 scene. (MWC)

As with others on the Norfolk & Suffolk Joint Railways Committee line, the station at Lowestoft North was quite large with full facilities including, in the winter, blazing fires in the Booking Hall and waiting rooms! Yarmouth South Town allocated Class C12 4-4-2T No. 67387 pauses at Lowestoft North station in 1954 with a Yarmouth bound train. Introduced in 1898, the Class C12 was a H.A. Ivatt design for the Great Northern Railway. Under the LNER and British Railways these locomotives were to be found at numerous locations in East Anglia. (NF)

During the last years of the former N&SJRC Yarmouth South Town to Lowestoft Central railway it was a single line throughout. The condition of Lowestoft North in this view, is typical of all stations on the line after the drastic reduction in the infrastructure which followed the withdrawal of the staff, goods facilities and the through trains. Corton, Hopton and Gorleston-on-Sea had similar substantial stations, once of great importance to the community. Unfortunately they soon became prime targets for vandals. The land previously occupied by Lowestoft North station and goods yard is now occupied by residential housing. This view of the station in 1970 is from the now demolished bridge carrying the A12 trunk road over the railway and looking north towards Great Yarmouth. (SJ)

Working in from Yarmouth Beach over the N&SJRC line, M&GNJR locomotives were regularly seen at Lowestoft. Often the trains were hauled by Class A 4-4-2 tank locomotives but other visitors included Class A 4-4-0 and D 0-6-0 locomotives. Class A 4-4-0 No. 24 is nicely positioned for the photographer in this scene at Lowestoft Central. (MWC)

In the years prior to the withdrawal of services between Yarmouth Beach and Lowestoft Central, motive power on the 11.15am passenger train service from Beach to Lowestoft and the corresponding return working was provided by Yarmouth Beach and often Ivatt 4MTs operated the train. No. 43090 is seen at Lowestoft Central waiting to return to Yarmouth Beach. Some other members of this versatile class recorded by the author at Lowestoft during 1952/53 include Nos. 43092, 43093, 43104, 43105, 43106, 43107, 43111, 43143 and the most regular, No. 43156. No. 43106 is preserved on the Severn Valley Railway. (NF)

Designed by T.W. Worsdell for the GER and later modified by J. Holden, the Class F4 2-4-2T locomotives were introduced in 1884. In later years they became a common sight, along with Class F5 and F6 locomotives, in Suffolk and Norfolk on local services. Frequently used on Yarmouth Beach and South Town services from Lowestoft, Class F4 No. 67174 is seen here in the sidings at Lowestoft in 1953. (NF)

Left - Another Lowestoft scene showing a former GER 2-4-2T locomotive. Class F6 No. 67231 was the last of the type to be allocated to Lowestoft and one of the last two working over the former N&SJRC line from Yarmouth South Town to Lowestoft. During 1957, Class F6 2-4-2Ts Nos. 67229 and 67231 worked afternoon trains over the coast line at a time when some other services were provided by diesel multiple units. These two were the last of their type allocated to engine sheds in East Norfolk and Suffolk. This 24th April 1957 scene shows No. 67231 waiting to leave platform four and go to Lowestoft engine sheds. *(MWC)* **Below**- Two views of steam hauled Yarmouth - London through trains recorded at Lowestoft when services ran via the coast line. On the left is Class 7MT 4-6-2 No. 70002 *Geoffrey Chaucer* and on the right Class B17/1 4-6-0 No. 61647 *Helmingham Hall. (BL)*

Diverting the Yarmouth - London trains via Lowestoft gave some stations such as Gorleston-on-Sea regular daily through services to the capital. However this arrangement was short lived and it would not be many years before Gorleston, with its greatly expanding population, business parks and a large district hospital, would be removed from the national rail network for ever. An English Electric Class 40 1Co-Co1 locomotive takes the line to Beccles at Oulton Broad with a train from Yarmouth South Town to Liverpool Street. (SJ)

A Brush Class 31 A1A-A1A diesel electric locomotive heads a Yarmouth South Town - London Liverpool Street train near Barnby, having reversed at Lowestoft. (SJ)

A superb view of Caister-on-Sea station showing a wonderful selection of posters advertising Midland Railway and Great Northern Railway travel opportunities from the station. Opened on 7th August 1877, Caister-on-Sea became one of the more important small stations on the line to Yarmouth Beach with trains from the Midlands, the North and London stopping there. Closed with the majority of the line on 28th February 1959, other uses were found for the building before it was finally demolished. The land previously occupied by the station is now used for housing, but in 2005 it is still possible to find evidence of the railway at Caister. (CTC)

During the summer of 1933, the Sentinel steam railcar *Tantivy* was used on a new service that ran between Yarmouth Beach and all the halts and stations on the M&GN as far as Stalham. Railway halts were built at Newtown, Caister Camp, California, Scratby, Little Ormesby, Potter Heigham and Sutton Staithe. Except for Caister Camp Halt, which was more substantial, these were low wooden platforms with little or no facilities. Surrounded by happy campers with more inside, *Tantivy* stands at Caister Camp Halt in 1933, the one year that the railcar was used on the service. It was stated at the time that *Tantivy* was on loan to the M&GNJR and normally worked from Whitby. By the end of 1933, the service had carried 22,276 passengers between 17th July and 9th September. (*CTC*)

A high summer view of Caister Camp Halt with two of the many Great Yarmouth Corporation tram bodies purchased by the camp for use as chalets. These two however appear to be in use as toilets. (*CTC*)

Designed by S. Holden for the GER and introduced in 1912, Class J19 0-6-0 locomotives were equally at home hauling goods or passenger trains. This view of Martham in 1949 shows No. 64653 with a local passenger train waiting to depart from the station. Opened on 15th July 1877, Martham station was situated between Hemsby and Potter Heigham and in fact the station was called Martham for Rollesby. This well used station closed on 28th February 1959. (*StationsUK*)

The suspension of rail services and the removal of the railway serving Great Yarmouth soon produced sights such as this along the closed line. Martham station on 15th July 1963 awaits the developers to move in. (*Photo Courtesy RCTS/W00L047*)

Situated further along the former M&GNJR towards Melton Constable, Catfield station was 15½ miles from Yarmouth Beach. The station and track bed looking towards Stalham is seen here on 15th July 1963 before any redevelopment had started. The location now forms part of the busy A149 Great Yarmouth to Cromer road.
(Photo Courtesy RCTS/W00L057)

In unusual lighting conditions, a heavy Birmingham New Street - Yarmouth Beach through train leaves North Walsham Town station behind Ivatt Class 4MT 2-6-0 No. 43158 in the summer of 1958. Much of the former railway land in this area is now used for roads including a long section of former trackbed between North Walsham and Honing and also between Stalham and Potter Heigham. No. 43158 was allocated to Yarmouth Beach for many years. *(FC)*

Designed by J. Holden for the GER and introduced in 1901, a number of Class J17 0-6-0 locomotives were allocated to sheds on the former M&GNJR including Yarmouth Beach. Their ability to cope with all types of work from heavy passenger to light goods duties made them a good multipurpose locomotive. On 8th August 1958 one of the class passes Aylsham North station with a short pick up goods. No sign of this station exists now and a road has replaced the trackbed almost up to the bridge, seen in the distance, which still exists. (FC)

Another view of a Class J17 0-6-0 at work on the former M&GNJR in 1958 with a pick up goods, but on this occasion at Corpusty and Saxthorpe. This station was located 36¾ miles from Yarmouth Beach and situated between Aylsham North and Melton Constable. One of this Class, No. 65567, is preserved as GER No. 1217 in the National Railway Collection at York. (FC)

Melton Constable was the heart of the M&GNJR and had a considerable allocation of motive power. In this view, M&GNJR Class D 0-6-0 No. 59 is seen in company with other M&GNJR locomotives along the side of the engine shed. Designed by S. Johnson and built in 1896, No. 59 was withdrawn in 1944.

These locomotives were of the standard Midland Railway Class 2F design, and carried the same boilers as the Class C 4-4-0s. (MWC)

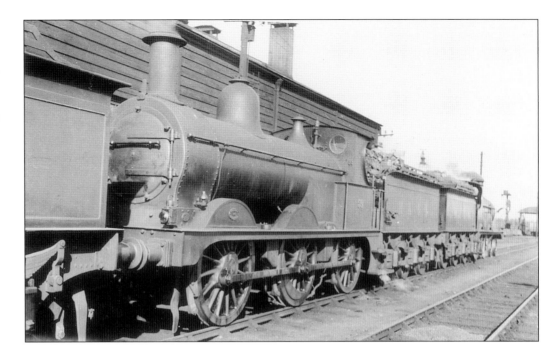

Completed in 1905 at Melton Constable, M&GNJR 0-6-0T No. 16 could be found in the yard there on 31st Oct 1934. This locomotive proved to be rather special since it was included in the British Railways stocklist as Class J93 0-6-0T No. 68489. It was withdrawn from service in August 1949. (MWC)

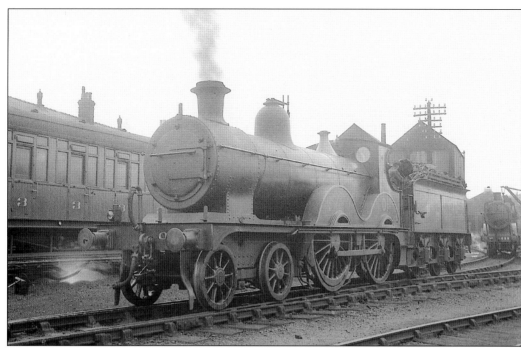

When the LNER took control in 1936, the M&GNJR locomotives were renumbered. M&GNJR Class C 4-4-0 No. 1 as LNER No. 01 was at Melton Constable on a fine day in 1937. The flower pot chimney was fitted in 1935.
(Photo Courtesy RCTS/DWA0092)

The 3rd August 1936 was rather overcast at Melton Constable where M&GNJR Class C 4-4-0 No. 47 is seen waiting to depart with a Yarmouth train. Within a few months changes would be put in place as the LNER took over the running of the M&GNJR and set about the replacement of much of the motive power used on the line. *(MWC)*

The summer of 1958 was to be the last for the direct line from Yarmouth Beach to the Midlands. At Melton Constable, Ivatt Class 4MT 2-6-0 No. 43110 of South Lynn shed passes with a short goods train, whilst a Metropolitan Cammell Class 101 diesel multiple unit forming a Norwich service waits in the platform. Passenger services finally ended at Melton Constable in 1964 with closure of the line to Sheringham. (MWC)

A number of Ivatt 4MT 2-6-0s were allocated to Yarmouth Beach, one of which was No. 43159. Having worked in from Yarmouth, the Class 4MT had just come off the turntable at Melton Constable when this scene was recorded in 1956. (DW)

Much publicity surrounded the running of the last passenger trains over the former M&GNJR. Another historic occasion was the arrival at Melton Constable of the last goods train from Yarmouth Beach. The train, headed by Ivatt 4MT 2-6-0 No. 43107, is seen here arriving at Melton Constable on Saturday 28th February 1959. *(HMRS/Seabrook Gibbs Coll'n)*

One of the regular Class B12/3 4-6-0s to work on the former M&GNJR in the 1950s, leaves Fakenham West station on 14th April 1952 with a Peterborough - Yarmouth Beach train. This particular locomotive, No. 61530, was allocated to Yarmouth Beach for many years, but in February 1959 was reallocated to Norwich and in June the same year moved to Cambridge. After withdrawal from service in November 1959, No. 61530 was immediately scrapped at Stratford. *(HMRS/E.S. Russell Coll'n)*

YARMOUTH SOUTH TOWN- IPSWICH (DIRECT)

Great Yarmouth suffered two major rail closures in 1959 and as a consequence the dismal scene of closed stations on once important rail links became common. Just outside Yarmouth and the first station on the main line to London, Belton and Burgh was one such station and is seen here on 15th July 1963.
(Photo Courtesy RCTS/W004064)

Back in 1911, Belton and Burgh station was very much the heart of village life and set amongst rolling countryside. No trace of the station exists today and since the location and some of surrounding countryside was designated for development, residential housing now covers much of the land seen here. *(HMRS/ H. F. Hilton Coll'n)*

The last day of direct through services between Yarmouth South Town and Liverpool Street was 2nd November 1959 and one of the last was hauled by Class B1 4-6-0 No. 61051. Here that train is approaching St. Olaves Swing Bridge. Through services continued via Lowestoft, but these finished in September 1966. This paved the way for the eventual complete closure of Yarmouth South Town (DW)

On 24th October 1959 Class B17/6 4-6-0 No. 61670 *City of London* runs into Haddiscoe High Level with an up train. Entering service as No. 2870 *Manchester City* on 13th May 1937, within days this was changed to *Tottenham Hotspur*. In 1937 a new express train was planned to run between Norwich and London which required two engines to be streamlined similarly to Gresley's Class A4 4-6-2s. One was No. 2870 which became Class B17/5 No. 2870 *City of London*. In the 1948 renumbered scheme, *City of London* became No. 61670 and in the early 1950s the streamlining was removed. Allocated to Yarmouth South Town for many years, *City of London* was withdrawn at Lowestoft in April 1960. *(Photo Courtesy RCTS/FAI0564)*

On the last day of services on the Yarmouth South Town - Beccles line, a train hauled by Class B1 4-6-0 No. 61051 is near Aldeby and heading for Beccles, the next stop. (DW)

Ipswich allocated Class B12/3 4-6-0 No. 61564 pauses at Beccles on 2nd March 1957 with a goods train from Yarmouth South Town. Designed by S. D. Holden as express passenger engines for the GER, the Class B12/3 was a Gresley rebuild. These locomotives were frequently seen at work on the East Suffolk line hauling Yarmouth trains. No. 61564 was withdrawn from service in November 1957 and cut up at Stratford in December 1958. It was one of several Class B12 locomotives at Ipswich. (DW)

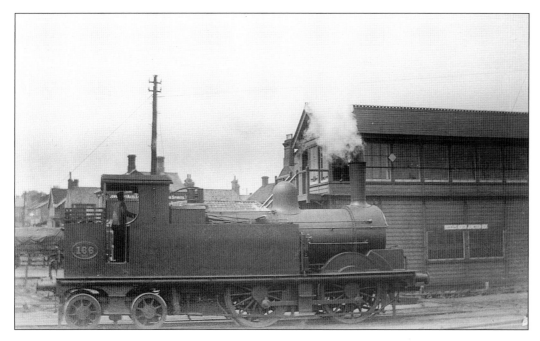

Beccles was once an important junction with railway lines leaving the town in four directions. One of the signal boxes at Beccles is seen here on 8th July 1901 together with Johnson designed GER 0-4-4T No. 166. Thirty of engines were built, with No. 166 being completed in 1873 by Neilson. The first 0-4-4s in England to be fitted with side tanks, they were later modified by Adams with the addition of a cab. Of interest is the fact that one of this class, No. 189, was the first GER engine to be painted in the blue livery adopted by the Company.

The sign advertising "Lowestoft Ales", seen through the cab of the engine is of historic interest. (*KN/LCGB*)

Gresley designed B17/6 4-6-0 No. 61665 *Leicester City* departs from Beccles with a London bound express. One of the regular engines on the East Suffolk and allocated to Yarmouth South Town for many years, *Leicester City* was withdrawn from traffic there in April 1959 and cut up at Doncaster works the following June. (*GM*)

Class D16/3 4-4-0 No. 62564 was a rebuilt Class D16/2 with round topped boiler, but retaining the original footplating and slide valves. On a warm August day in 1953 it was at Beccles with a local train from Yarmouth South Town. With the increased availability of Ivatt 4MT 2-6-0 locomotives for use on the former M&GNJR, No. 62564 had been reallocated the previous year from Yarmouth Beach to Norwich. (DW)

With the increasing use of diesel motive power on routes previously steam operated with Britannia Class 7MT 4-6-2 locomotives, their appearance on the Yarmouth South Town - London services became common both on the direct route and, after November 1959, on services via Lowestoft. Stratford's No. 70034 *Thomas Hardy* is seen here on the East Suffolk line with a Yarmouth South Town - Lowestoft - London Liverpool Street service. (MWC)

THE EASTERLING

LONDON (Liverpool Street)

AND

LOWESTOFT AND YARMOUTH

WEEKDAYS

	S a.m.	E a.m.			
London (Liverpool Street) ...dep	10 33	11 3			p.m.
	p.m.	p.m.	Yarmouth (South Town) ... ...dep		7 10
			Lowestoft (Central) ... ... „		7 10
Beccles... ... ...arr	12 57	1 18			
Lowestoft (Central) ... „	1 24	1 45	Beccles ... ... „		7 35
Yarmouth (South Town) ... „	1 22	1 42	London (Liverpool Street)... ... ...arr		10 0

E Except Saturdays   S Saturdays only

Refreshment Cars available between London (Liverpool Street) and Yarmouth (South Town).

Passengers travelling from London (Liverpool Street), Lowestoft (Central) and Yarmouth (South Town) by this service can reserve seats in advance on payment of a fee of 1s. 0d. per seat.

"The Easterling", a priority named train, was introduced for the summer timetable in 1950 to provide a non-stop fast service between London, Great Yarmouth and Lowestoft, stopping only at the important junction station of Beccles. On the left is an extract from the named trains section of the 1952 British Railways summer timetable and on the right is a superb view of the "The Easterling" on the East Suffolk line headed by Stratford allocated Thompson Class B1 4-6-0 No. 61336. (MWC)

The Yarmouth - London expresses no longer pass through Woodbridge, but this view takes us back to those days when it was common to see a Class B17 4-6-0 locomotive and train at the station. No. 61647 *Helmingham Hall*, a Class B17/1, has just arrived at Woodbridge and is waiting to recommence the journey to Yarmouth South Town. Completed in August 1935 as LNER No. 2847 *Helmingham Hall*, it later became British Railways No. 61647 and in 1958 was rebuilt as a Class B17/6. It was withdrawn from traffic in November 1959 and cut up at Doncaster in March 1960. Woodbridge is a busy station and since 2004 has been served by the regular two hourly direct services between Lowestoft and London operated by Class 170 units, as well as local services. (*SLS*)

D16/3 4-4-0 No. 62546 *Claud Hamilton* was perhaps Yarmouth South Town's most celebrated locomotive. Allocated there for many years, it was usually kept in a superb condition as seen here at Woodbridge whilst working an Ipswich - Yarmouth South Town stopping train. (*MWC*)

The East Suffolk line station at Westerfield is 72 miles 18 chains from London Liverpool Street, and is the junction for the Felixstowe branch. An express for Yarmouth South Town headed by LNER B17/1 4-6-0 No. 2806 *Audley End* is seen passing through the station in the early 1930s. Included in the train would be carriages destined for Lowestoft, which would be detached from the main train at Beccles. Passenger rail services through Westerfield today consist of local services between Ipswich and Felixstowe, Saxmundham and Lowestoft, and the London through services to and from Lowestoft. Other regular traffic passing through Westerfield are the many container trains to the port at Felixstowe and the trains serving the nuclear power station at Sizewell. No. 2806 was built in 1928, renumbered LNER No. 1606 in 1946 and renumbered British Railways No. 61606 in 1948. Rebuilt as a Class B17/6 in 1950, No. 61606 was withdrawn from traffic in 1958, and cut up at Doncaster in January 1959. (*PTP*)

A view of GER Holden designed oil fired Class P43 4-2-2 No. 14 taking on fuel at Ipswich. This handsome locomotive was built in 1898 and scrapped in 1907, the short life being attributed to the 7ft. driving wheels being unable to provide enough adhesion to cope with the longer and heavier passenger trains being introduced in the early 1900s. The class consisted of ten locomotives and were the last GER "singles". (KN/LCGB)

The former GER "Claud Hamilton" 4-4-0s passed through a number of rebuilding programmes during their lives and eventually became a common sight at all Great Yarmouth stations. No. 1884 is seen here leaving Ipswich with an express for South Town in GER days. This engine was rebuilt in 1922, 1928 and finally as a Class D16/3 in 1943. In the British Railways numbering scheme it became No. 62515. Withdrawal from service came in April 1958, the last years of the life of No. 62515 being spent allocated to Melton Constable from where it no doubt visited Yarmouth Beach. (MWC)

Class B17/6 No. 61670 *City of London* bursts out of Ipswich Tunnel with an express for Yarmouth South Town and Lowestoft. For many years allocated to Yarmouth South Town, *City of London* was withdrawn from Lowestoft in 1960. It had been transferred there after the closure of the Yarmouth South Town - Beccles line in 1959 and the rerouting of the Yarmouth South Town - London services via Lowestoft. (*MWC*)

After being displaced from the Liverpool Street - Norwich expresses by diesel locomotives, the Britannia Class 7MT 4-6-2 locomotives became a common sight on the East Suffolk main line to Yarmouth South Town. Arriving at Ipswich with the afternoon van train from Yarmouth is No. 70041 *Sir John Moore*. Other locomotives to be used on this train included Classes B1, B12/3, B17 and D16/3.(*JH/EMJ*)

The view from a London Liverpool Street train waiting to depart from Ipswich and enter the Tunnel. (*SJ*)

An express for Liverpool Street headed by newly built LNER Class B17/1 4-6-0 No. 2838 *Melton Hall* emerges from Ipswich Tunnel in 1933. Rebuilt in December 1958 as a Class B17/6, *Melton Hall* was withdrawn from traffic in March 1958, and cut up the following May at Doncaster. It had spent many years allocated to March(31B). (*RAS*)

LNER Class B12/1 4-6-0 No. 1518E heads an express for the east coast from London Liverpool Street. Originating from a GER Holden design of 1911, the majority of the Class B12 locomotives were rebuilt as Class B12/3. (*MWC*)

Whilst a review of the London - Ipswich part of the journey to Yarmouth is not for this book, having been already covered in another in this series, an exception has been made for this fine print of "The Easterling" waiting to leave London Liverpool Street with coaches for Yarmouth South Town and Lowestoft. Stratford's Britannia Class 7MT 4-6-2 No. 70036 *Boadicea* is heading the train, the main part of which would go to Yarmouth South Town after running non-stop to Beccles, and leaving the Lowestoft coaches there. These would be taken forward to Lowestoft usually by a local tank engine such as a Class L1, N7, C12, F4, F5 or F6. (*Photo Courtesy RCTS/CRA0146*)

These fine historic images show Breydon Junction together with the once important signal box, where the two lines serving Great Yarmouth converge. **Top Left**-View from the signal box towards Yarmouth. **Top Right**-View from the signal box with the Reedham line on the left and the Acle line on the right. **Bottom Left**-View towards the signal box and Yarmouth with the Reedham line on the right. **Bottom Right**-View towards the signal box with the Reedham line on the left and the Acle line just visible on the right. (*GM*)

'one' Railway operated Anglia Railways liveried Class 150/2 diesel multiple unit No. 150213 *Lord Nelson*, approaches Reedham from Berney Arms whilst working a Yarmouth - Norwich service. The double track line to Lowestoft is on the right. At the time of writing (mid 2005), 'one' plans to replace these units, which were built in York and introduced in 1987, with more comfortable Class 156 units. (*MW*)

A view through the rear windows of a dmu standing in the up platform at Reedham showing in the distance, a failed Class 104 dmu on the right and on the left, a Class 37 diesel electric locomotive sent out to retrieve the failure. Both the Class 37 and the failed dmu have been placed off the up and down lines to minimise further delays to services. Reedham is 12¼ miles from Norwich and the junction of the Lowestoft line and the original Norwich & Yarmouth Railway which opened on 1st May 1844. (*GM*)

The second and shorter route between Yarmouth and Norwich opened on 1st June 1883 with intermediate stations at Acle and Lingwood. This is Acle station after a heavy snowfall with a Cravens Class 105 dmu forming a Norwich - Yarmouth service. (*GM*)

The junction at Brundall is where the line to Yarmouth, which opened in 1883, joins the original 1844 line which runs via Reedham. Brundall station is seen here following heavy snow which had earlier blocked lines in the area. A Norwich train formed of a Cravens Class 105 dmu runs into the station in this early 1980s scene. (*GM*)

To celebrate the centenary of the opening of the Yarmouth - Acle - Lingwood - Brundall line, on the 1st June 1983, a special Pullman train was arranged which left Great Yarmouth at 1920hrs and then proceeded to Acle and Lingwood. It was scheduled to arrive back at Yarmouth at 2221hrs. **Top Left** - The train at Acle with crowds on the platform. **Top Right** - The train, which is seen here at Lingwood, was hauled by Brush Class 31/4 A1A-A1A No. 31405 a locomotive that started life as No. D5606. **Bottom Right** - Prior to departure of the train from Yarmouth, a gathering of civic leaders gave their support for the occasion. (*CTC*)

East of Norwich, Thorpe is a familiar location to thousands of Great Yarmouth, Lowestoft, Cromer and Sheringham rail users who travel daily on the Norwich services.
A Metropolitan-Cammell diesel multiple unit crosses one of the river bridges there whilst working a Yarmouth service in this 1960 scene. The first of this type of unit entered service in 1956-57. Unit E79042/E79258 was recorded working Yarmouth services on 26th January 1957. (MWC)

Headed by GER Sharp Stewart 2-4-0 No. 30 the 8.6am Kings Lynn-Yarmouth Vauxhall train arrives at Norwich Thorpe on 15th April 1911. Introduced in 1867, this class consisted of 40 locomotives, all of which were scrapped between 1901 and 1913. (KN/LCGB)

A three coach local service from Yarmouth via Reedham arrives at Norwich at 1.24pm on 29th August 1959 headed by Thompson Class L1 2-6-4 No. 67705. This locomotive, one of a class of 100, was allocated to Ipswich for many years and used extensively on Felixstowe services. A Brush Type 2 locomotive is on the right. The Laurence Scott & Electromotors factory, a well known feature of the local scene, is on the left. This was later demolished and the site developed for housing.
(HMRS/Seabrook Gibbs Coll'n)

A typical scene in the 1950s at Norwich with Class D16/3 4-4-0 No. 62511 waiting to depart with a van train. This locomotive was a Gresley rebuild of a Class D15 with larger round topped boiler and modified footplating. *(SJ)*

Lowestoft's Class K3 2-6-0 No. 61959 leaves Norwich for Yarmouth Vauxhall at 11.57am on 29th August 1959 with a London Liverpool Street -Yarmouth Vauxhall through train. With the closure of the Yarmouth South Town - Beccles line and loss of the direct route to London for Yarmouth trains later that year, this scene of a train between Yarmouth and London routed via Norwich would in future become the norm. *(HMRS/Seabrook Gibbs Coll'n)*

Diesel electric Brush Type 2 A1A-A1A No. D5532 leaves Norwich with a local service for Yarmouth Vauxhall at 1.40pm on 29th August 1959 with the same carriages that had arrived a few minutes earlier behind Class L1 2-6-4 No. 67705. Diesel motive power was making serious inroads into steam operations at that time. Under the numerical renumbering scheme in the late 1960s, No. D5532 was renumbered No. 31114. The one time Laurence Scott & Electromotors factory is on the right. *(HMRS/Seabrook Gibbs Coll'n)*

Through trains between coastal resorts and major inland cities such as Sheffield, York, Leicester, Birmingham and Manchester have been a feature of railway timetables in the past. In recent years only the through services to London have run from East Anglian resorts, but in 1957 scenes such as this at Caister-on-Sea were common. Class D16/3 4-4-0 No. 62517 crosses the level crossing there and brings the Yarmouth Beach - Birmingham train into the station. (PTP)

Twenty-one years earlier in August 1936, the Birmingham -Yarmouth Beach train was double headed by LMS Class 2P 4-4-0 No. 542 and LMS Class 4F No. 4032. The LMS Class 4F 0-6-0s continued to venture as far as Yarmouth Beach into the 1950s on summer Saturday workings. (HJ/CR)

Further motive power variety in the shape of LNER Class D9 4-4-0 No. 6018 is featured here on a Birmingham - Yarmouth Beach train in June 1946. (HJ/CR)

Complete with offset smoke box door, large GNR boiler, large raised brass numerals on the cab, and M&GN on the lined-out tender, Class Da 0-6-0 No. 89 provides another fine example of motive power found on the rail network leading to Yarmouth Beach in 1936. No. 89 was one of a batch of 12 locomotives delivered to the M&GNJR in 1901, all of which later had extended smoke boxes fitted and were reboilered with the type of boiler seen here. An LMS class 4F can be seen in the background. (HJ/CR)

An up express headed by Class B17/6 4-6-0 No. 61659 *East Anglian* and Class B1 4-6-0 No. 61048 approaches St. Olaves swing bridge in September 1958. *(EA/CR)*

Gresley designed Class B17/6 4-6-0 No. 61611 *Raynham Hall* passes Belton with an up express in September 1958. Entering service as LNER No. 2811 in August 1930, *Raynham Hall* was withdrawn from service at Norwich in October 1959 and scrapped at Doncaster in February 1960. *(EA/CR)*

The through trains between Yarmouth South Town and London Liverpool Street produced a fine selection of main line locomotives with many classes including B1, B12/3, D16/3, Britannia's and the new diesel electric Type 2s at work on the line. Scenes such as this between St. Olaves and Haddiscoe with two B17/6 4-6-0s Nos. 61659 *East Anglian* and No. 61664 *Liverpool* double heading an up service made an impression on one, and how lucky those of us who witnessed it were. *(EA/CR)*

Norwich allocated diesel multiple unit formation No. 30 comprised Cravens built Class 105 Driving Motor Brake Second No. 53359 and Driving Trailer Second (L) No. 54122, both dating from 1956. Towards the end of the life of this unit it received special treatment when it was restored to the condition in which it first entered service. The work included all seats being recovered, the entire floor recovered in dark blue linoleum and all ceilings and walls washed and redecorated were necessary. The smart unit is seen here at Yarmouth Vauxhall on 5th July 1986 whilst working a Norwich service. *(NF)*

Colour views of the daily goods train on the former N&SJRC line between Yarmouth South Town and Lowestoft hauled by diesel electric locomotives are quite rare. With the full infrastructure still in place, the goods is seen heading for Lowestoft hauled by Brush Type 2 AlA AlA No. D5557. Freight services ceased completely on the line in November 1967. Under the renumbering scheme this locomotive became No. 31139. (PK)

With track rationalisation and unstaffed stations, the Yarmouth - Lowestoft line became a basic railway. The hybrid diesel multiple unit, so familiar to regular users of the line, is seen here providing an afternoon Yarmouth - Lowestoft service in the last few months of the lines existence. This location is now a dual carriageway road. (PK)

There is much more to a railway than trains, and long demolished signal boxes and other aspects of the infrastructure have their own special appeal. Another very rare colour image of the Yarmouth railway scene is provided by this view of the signal box at South Town. (*PK*)

At Gorleston, an interesting reminder of the past was provided by this trackside sign. "N&SJR" cast iron signs of this type were never common and this particular superb example was smashed one night by a "collector" trying to remove it. (*PK*)

NSJR   NOTICE
ANY PERSON FOUND TRESPASSING
OR THROWING RUBBISH OF ANY
KIND ON TO THE RAILWAY COMPANY'S
PROPERTY WILL BE PROSECUTED
Q.32

Diesel Electric Class 47/4 Co-Co No. 47522 leaves Vauxhall with a summer cross-country service consisting of Mark I stock. No doubt prepared for a special occasion, this scene shows how attractive a diesel locomotive can look when care and attention has been taken in preparing it for duty. No. 47522 was originally No. D1105. (GM)

At one time the Metropolitan Cammell Class 101 and Cravens Class 105 diesel multiple units were the mainstay of local services throughout East Anglia. Today, to travel in one of these units is a great attraction to many railway enthusiasts. The author of this work made hundreds of daily journeys in Class 101 and 105 units and in their last years of service they were anything but an attraction! Failures were common due to servicing difficulties and many had broken or ripped seats, faulty or broken windows and a generally dirty interior. It seemed that Norwich Depot got the units that nobody else wanted! Norwich diesel multiple unit formation No. 37 is seen here leaving Vauxhall for Norwich. (GM)

An ongoing local problem appears to be the lack of diesel multiple units and at the time of writing (2005) the problem remains with hauled trains being used occasionally as substitutes on services to Yarmouth. The reasons for the shortage may be different, but this situation is not new and on 20th August 1994, English Electric Class 37/0 Co-Co No. 37109 was used with spare coaches from Norwich Crown Point to provide Yarmouth travellers with a higher standard of comfort than would normally be the case. Here we see the Class 37 waiting to leave Norwich for Yarmouth. At the time of writing this English, Welsh & Scottish Railways locomotive is stored. (MW)

On another occasion the non-availability of diesel multiple units lead to Brush Class 47/7 Co-Co No. 47715 *Haymarket* being used to maintain Yarmouth's rail services. The Network South East liveried modified 100mph Type 4 is seen here bathed in the early morning sunshine waiting to depart from Norwich with a Yarmouth train made up of four spare inter city coaches. In 2005, this locomotive is owned by Fragonset Railways. (MW)

YARMOUTH RAILWAY MEMORIES

Mr. R. G. E. Castleton

I was born and bred in Colville Road, Oulton Broad and my schooling started at Dell Road School. I used to walk over the level crossings in Victoria Road from Dell Road and therefore occasionally saw the goods train heading for the Kirkley goods coal depot and the other lines in that area. There was a sandy area on the shores of Lake Lothing and my mates and I used to swim in the lake when the tide was right. Many times I did foolish things like climbing the railway embankment and putting dead fish on the track - only to be told off by the signalman from the swing bridge signal box, if and when he caught us! Little did I realise that after leaving Alderman Woodrow Secondary Boys School at 15, and starting a railway career, that one day I would be cleaning and firing large steam locomotives.

My railway career started in April 1955 at March Depot in Cambridgeshire and finished at Stratford Depot in East London in October 1997. I remember quite distinctly firing Class B1 4-6-0 No. 61043 one Saturday morning, but the year escapes me. I was at March Depot and my duty that day was to travel as "passenger" with my driver (J. Banks) to Great Yarmouth.

We were to work the 10.00am Yarmouth - Nottingham summer holiday express return. On arrival at Yarmouth Vauxhall our loco, No. 61043, was all ready at the head of the train. A more grimy-looking locomotive it was hard to imagine but looks can be deceiving! We left the station 10 minutes late and headed for Norwich and the Wensum Curve. No. 61043 steamed and rode exceptionally well. Booked to stop at Brandon to top up with water, my driver said that as we were running 10 minutes late we would try to get to Peterborough North without this stop. He told me not to waste steam through the safety valves, nor whilst working the injectors replacing water in the boiler. On arrival at Peterborough North we unhooked to allow for a Midland Region engine to take the train forward. We then ran "light engine" (LE) to the station at Peterborough East, into the depot and onto the turntable in preparation for running LE to March depot. With the locomotive turned, we stopped at the water crane to fill the tender. As I opened the tender water tank lid the tank was beginning to dry out!

A truly amazing demonstration of the art of driving and firing a steam locomotive as economically as possible and also of making up lost time. Being a fireman on that day was made easy for me by the driver who was a very good engineman. The distance was in excess of 100 miles and we covered it non-stop from Great Yarmouth to Peterborough North.

Thompson designed Class B1 4-6-0 No. 61043 which was the locomotive hauling the train from Yarmouth to Peterborough featured in Fireman Castleton's story. For many years this engine was allocated to Norwich. (DWC)

Mr. Jim Higgins

My father was a Londoner, who joined the LNER in the 1930s at Liverpool Street (his father worked on the GER at Bishopsgate) and learned his trade as a blockman and a traffic operator with Montgomery's 21st Army Group in World War II.

After the war he became a booking clerk at **Yarmouth Vauxhall** and, using his operating experience, did relief work as stationmaster in the summer (Darsham, Brampton, Aldeby, Belton, Homersfield, Lingwood, Whitlingham, Somerleyton, Corton and Hopton spring to mind and there may be several others that escape me). In the mid 1950s, the Yarmouth Mercury did a feature on Vauxhall and published a picture of the parcels/left luggage office on a peak summer Saturday, with my father well to the fore in an appropriate pose! When it came my turn to work at Vauxhall, I spent most of my time buried deep in the Goods Office.

It is hard to imagine **Yarmouth Beach** station on a busy summer Saturday with myself answering a non-stop stream of questions such as "When's next train to Chesterfield duck"? ......"When does train get to Nottingham…..Derby…..etc. All the time I would be heaving left luggage over the counter and slapping a new ticket on it, this was because I was young, (the old sweats would slap used tickets on it if they could). Never been more knackered in my life and now it is a car park!

Yarmouth South Town I remember less for working there than for catching the early morning train to Haddiscoe where, amongst other things, I used to bike along the spur to Fleet Junction with the single line working staff, or across the swing bridge to St. Olaves box. The train was probably Class F5 or F6 2-4-2T hauled and I remember reading in the News Chronicle about the Suez invasion or the Hungarian uprising on the way to work. In the early 1960s, I spent two years at Blackwall Goods in London's dockland and by then the London Liverpool Street - Yarmouth trains went via Lowestoft. After a weekend back home, biking to South Town from near the race course and catching the earliest Monday morning train at some unearthly hour meant I missed most of the trip to Gorleston, Lowestoft, Beccles and was more often than not, still asleep when we got to Halesworth!

An LNER consignment note issued to E. Scarles of Nelson Road on 7th November 1931 at Yarmouth for the carriage of 22 boxes of kippers and bloaters to Derby.

Providing direct rail access between the port, many industrial premises and the national rail network, the quayside goods line was a valuable asset to Great Yarmouth. With the buildings of South Quay in the background, new 0-6-0 diesel shunter No. 11101 is seen on the quayside in May 1952 when it was officially allocated to Yarmouth South Town. The author of this work was fortunate in experiencing a cab ride in this locomotive along the tramway in that year. Initially designated Class DJ12 by British Railways, this type of locomotive later became known as Class 04. (MWC)

Before being replaced by diesel locomotives the motive power on the line was the much celebrated "Tram Locos", the Class J70 0-6-0T locomotives. Designed by J. Holden and introduced in 1903, these are easily recognised by children in the 21st century as "Toby" in the Thomas series of railway adventures. Ironically the diesel shunters that replaced the Class J70s also feature in the world famous Thomas series. No. 68219 is seen heading a goods train along one of the road sections of the line in 1951, and passing the offices and store of the well known brewer Steward & Patterson. (*StationsUK*)

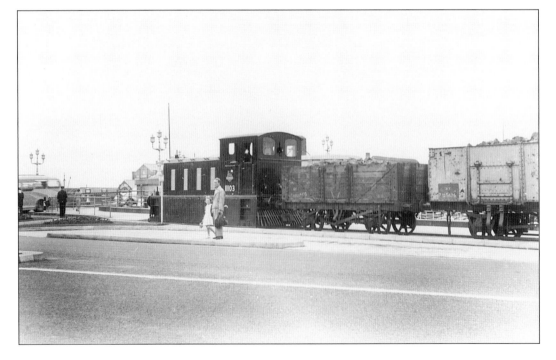

Replacement for the Class J70 locomotives came in 1952 when the diesel mechanical 0-6-0 shunters of the Class DJ12 arrived. With enclosed motion, class member No. 11103 is about to stop the traffic crossing Haven Bridge and then make for the port area. Powered by a Gardner 8L3 engine these locomotives were nominally rated at 200hp. (*StationsUK*)

The quayside tramway could be accessed directly from Vauxhall station yard and via the Yarmouth Union Railway(YUR) from Beach station. In addition to allowing goods to pass between the quayside, riverside properties, the Fishwharf, and the railway network at Beach station, coal sidings and yards were established along the YUR. This view is looking north and shows some of these sidings. Others existed the other side of the crossing gates. The facilities afforded by the YUR remained open after the closure of Beach station, with access being maintained by the tramway from Vauxhall. The YUR finally closed in May 1970. (MWC)

At the southern end of the YUR, the line passed between the White Swan public house and a small gatehouse to gain access to the tramway. This is the view in the opposite direction to that seen above. The White Swan is on the right and the gatehouse on the left. The large building in the distance is Lacons brewery store which was demolished and is now the location of the Aldi supermarket. The White Swan survives today, but little else remains of this scene with major road changes in the North Quay area having a substantial impact on the environment. (CTC)

The railway line emerging from between the White Swan public house and gatehouse No. 50. In later years the railway trucks destined for the coal merchants were taken there from Vauxhall yard by a Class O4 0-6-0 diesel shunter, which was able to get through the gap between the buildings. The line in the foreground is crossing North Quay. *(PTP)*

Used initially on the Wisbech and Upwell Tramway but found to be unsuitable for that line, the Sentinel Wagon Works designed double ended tram engines were transferred to Great Yarmouth for use on the tramway there. Two of these unusual locomotives, LNER Class Y10 Nos. 8403 and 8404 are seen here in the yard at Vauxhall. In the 1943 renumbering scheme they became Nos. 7775 and 7776 and under the 1948 BR renumbering, they were given the Nos. 8186 and 8187.*(MWC)*

Looking south along the river from the roof of the municipal buildings in 1962, the major advantage of the railway tramway link is obvious. Large, bulky and heavy loads could be dispatched or received in the centre of the town and in the port area from the rail network. Today no sign of this valuable asset exists and all goods and freight goes by road through the town. The quayside is seen to be busy with several general cargo ships in port, at a time when the offshore oil and gas industry was only just beginning in Great Yarmouth with the first surveys being carried out in the North Sea. (*Archant*)

A 1936 view of Sentinel No. 8404 in the roadway at North Quay. The premises of a valuable railway customer and well known Yarmouth brewer, E. Lacon & Co. Ltd., can be seen on the left. *(Courtesy RCTS/ DWA0208)*

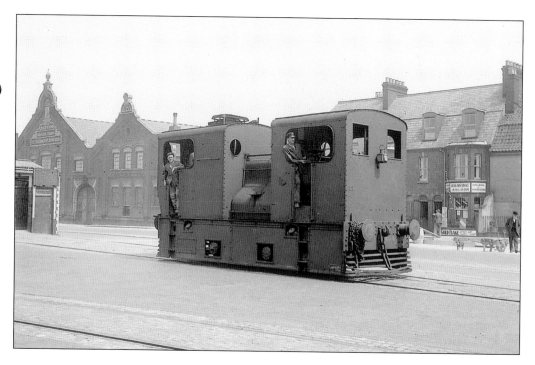

Being on the front line, Great Yarmouth suffered badly in the Second World War with very frequent air raids. One of the casualties of a German raid in July 1942 was the rail connected bottling store of Lacons brewery mentioned in the previous caption. The railway connected building is seen here immediately after the war with the tramway entering the building. *(CTC)*

A splendid view of one of the Sentinels heading back to Vauxhall on 8th July 1947 after a trip along the tramway to the quay and possibly the Fishwharf. Large quantities of coal and timber were unloaded from ships at Great Yarmouth in addition to huge quantities of fish, these were dispatched by the tramway to customers via Yarmouth Vauxhall and the national railway network. (*MWC*)

The London and North Western Railway (LNWR) booking and enquiry office on the Fish Wharf was an interesting aspect of the tramway. It is seen here complete with posters encouraging rail passengers to travel "The Royal Way" to Scotland. No doubt this was aimed at the thousands of Scottish workers involved in the herring industry who travelled by rail each autumn to East Anglia as the great herring shoals moved south with the fishing fleets and their support workers following. Other railway operators also had offices in the vicinity of the fish wharf. The Fish Wharf Post Office is the centre of this photograph and the LNWR office is on the left. The date is 19th January 1915 after the buildings had been damaged by German bombing. (*CTC*)

A photograph that tells much about booming Great Yarmouth in the 1950s. In addition to sending insulated containers by road to Vauxhall and South Town stations for despatch by rail, when there was sufficient demand Birds Eye used the tramway to despatch large amounts of their products in bulk direct from near their premises to the national rail network for distribution. With diesel shunters at the front and rear the Birds Eye train holds the traffic up as it crosses the road leading to the bridge. Other goods carried by the tramway such as timber and coal are to be seen in the trucks centre left. In addition to Birds Eye and the railway tramway, many other features of Yarmouth's great past are captured in this photograph including the Corporation buses, pleasure steamers and the impressive Breydon Bridge. It is August 1959. (*Archant*)

Diesel shunter Class 04 0-6-0 No. D2212 prepares to return to Vauxhall yard on 26th August 1959 after working in the quayside and port area. Amongst the goods wagons returning to Vauxhall are empty cattle trucks. The tramway closed in December 1975 and, as part of a major regeneration project of the South Quay area, all the railway track was removed. *(HMRS/Seabrook Gibbs Coll'n)*

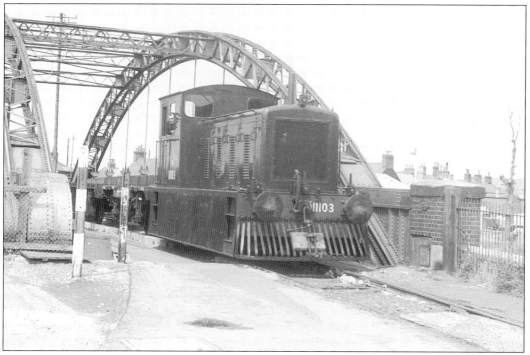

Perhaps the most memorable sight of the tramway was a locomotive coming over the bridge which spans the River Bure. Diesel mechanical Class DJ12 0-6-0 No. 11103 is seen crossing the bridge in the mid 1950s. The bridge remains in use as a footbridge in 2005. *(HMRS/Seabrook Gibbs Coll'n)*

Subject	Page
Acle	
View of station with Class 105 dmu	92
Special Train in platform	93
Aldeby	
View from train	80
Aylsham	
North Station with BR Class J17 loco.	73
Barnby	
BR Class 31 diesel loco.	68
Beccles	
BR loco. No. 61564	80
GER loco. No. 166 and BR loco. No. 61665	81
BR loco. No. 62564	82
Belton	
BR loco. No. 61867	Cover
BR loco. No. 61611	99
Belton and Burgh	
Station Views	78
Berney Arms	
Station view with dmu	Cover
Breydon Junction	
Signal box views	90
Brundall	
View of station with Class 105 dmu	92
Caister	
Station View	69
Camp Station View and Steam Railcar *Tantivy*	70
BR loco. No. 62517	97
Catfield	
Station View (Disused)	72
Corpusty and Saxthorpe	
Station view with BR Class J17 loco.	73
Fakenham	
West station with BR loco. No. 61530	77
Haddiscoe	
High Level station view with BR loco. No. 61670	79
Hopton	
Station view with BR Class C12 loco.	64
Gorleston	
Station view with BR loco. No. 67218	61
BR loco. No. 64643	61
Bridge view of BR dmu and Class 37 diesel loco.	62
Station view with BR Class 24 diesel loco.	63
BR Class 31 diesel loco. with weed killing train	63
Lineside view of dmu	Cover, 101
BR diesel loco. No. D5557	101
BR Class 31 diesel loco.	Cover
Steam Shovel and 1974 Station View	114
Ipswich	
GER locos. No. 14 and No. 1884	86
BR locos. No. 61670 and 70041	87
View of Tunnel and LNER loco. No. 2838	88
Lingwood	
Special train with BR diesel loco No. 31405	93
London	
Liverpool Street	
"The Easterling" and BR loco. No. 70036	89
Lowestoft	
Central	
M&GN loco. No. 24	65
BR loco. No. 43090	66
BR loco. No. 67174	66
BR loco. No. 67231	67

Subject	Page
North	
BR loco. No. 67387	64
Basic railway general view	65
Martham	
Station View with BR loco. No. 64653	71
Station view (Disused)	71
Melton Constable	
M&GN JR Locos. No. 16 and 59	74
LNER loco. No. 01 and M&GN loco. No. 47	75
Station view with BR loco. No. 43110 and dmu	76
BR loco. No. 43159	76
BR loco. No. 43107	77
North Walsham	
Town station view with BR loco No. 43158	72
Norwich	
GER loco. No. 30	94
BR locos. Nos. 67705 and 62511	95
BR loco. No. 61959 and diesel loco. No. D5532	96
BR diesel locos. Nos. 37109 and 47715	104
Diesel multiple unit on bridge at Thorpe	94
Oulton Broad	
BR Loco. Class 40 diesel loco.	68
Reedham	
View of junction with Class 150 dmu	91
View of station from inside dmu	91
St. Olaves	
BR loco. No. 61656	Cover
View from train	79
BR locos Nos. 61659 and 61048	99
BR locos Nos. 61659 and 61664	100
Westerfield	
LNER loco No. 2806	85
Woodbridge	
BR loco. No. 61668	1
BR locos. No. 62546 and 61647	84
Yarmouth	
Beach	
Withdrawal Notice	17
EMR loco. No. 43A and M&GN loco. No. 30	18
M&GN locos. Nos. 20 and 41	19
EMR loco. No. 26 and M&GN loco. No. 1	20
M&GN loco. No. 12 and station building from road	21
M&GN loco. No. 80	22
Scotch girls and platform view	23
M&GN loco. No. 80 and goods entrance	24
M&GN locos. Nos. 41 and 68	25
LNER locos. Nos. 06 and 4015	26
LNER loco. No. 4327	27
Platform view with BR loco. No. 62517	27
Platform view with BR loco. No. 43148	28
End of platform view with BR Class B12/3 loco.	28
Platform view with BR Class D16/3 loco.	29
BR diesel loco. No. 11174	29
Platform view with BR Class B12/3 loco.	30
Platform view	30
Engine sheds and BR loco. No. 43160	31
Views of Yarmouth Beach after closure	32
Views of Yarmouth Beach after closure	33
South Town	
BR loco. No. 70030	4
BR loco. No. 70000	13
Views of station building	34, 35

Subject	Page
Views of station interior	36, 38
Track level view of platform, train and building	36
LNER loco. No. 2813 on turntable	37
View of Engine Shed and track	38
BR loco. No. 61665	39
BR locos. Nos. 61622 and 61572	40
LNER loco. No. 7415 and BR loco. No. 67218	41
BR loco. No. 62553	42
BR locos. Nos. 65390 and No. 61664	43
BR Class 31 diesel locos	44
BR loco. No. 69690 with dmu	44
BR diesel loco. No. D5523 and dmu	45
Derelict platform views with dmu	46
1870s platform view with early loco.	47
Signal Box	102
Vauxhall	
External view of building in 1950s	48
External view of station with tram	49
External view of station in 2005	49
LNER loco. No. 7158 and station internal view	50
GER loco. No. 447	51
BR Loco. No. 67736 and 1924 platform view	52
BR Locos. Nos. 62517 with 62613	53
General view of station and yard from bridge	53
Internal view of station in 1950s with dmu	54
BR diesel locos. Nos. 31117 with 31271	54
BR diesel locos. Nos. 25134 with 25278	55
BR Class 47/4 diesel loco.	55
BR diesel locos. Nos. 31417 and 37054	56
BR heating unit (Class 31) and Class 47/4 loco	57
BR diesel locos Nos. 31407 and 47573	58
BR diesel loco. No. 37895 and coach derailment	59
Civic leaders on concourse	93
BR Class 105 Norwich No. 30 dmu	100
BR diesel loco. No. 47522	103
BR Class 105 Norwich No. 37 dmu	103
Railway Tramway	
BR diesel loco. No. 11101	107
BR loco. No. 68219 and diesel loco. No. 11103	108
Yarmouth Union Railway	109,110
LNER locos Nos. 8403 with 8404	110
General view of quay area (South)	111
LNER loco No. 8404 in road and Lacons Store	112
LNER Class Y10 0-4-0T loco.	113
LNWR Fishwharf Office	113
General view of Haven Bridge area	114
BR diesel locos. Nos. 11103 and No. D2212	115
Miscellaneous	
Birmingham-Yarmouth Beach Trains	
LMS loco. No. 4419	Cover
LMS locos No. 542 and 4032	97
LNER loco. No. 6018	98
East Suffolk Line	
BR. loco. No. 61670	3
"The Easterling" and BR loco. No. 61336	83
BR Loco. No. 70035	82
Others	
Rail Network Map	6
Bure Bridge and Breydon Viaduct	60
Yarmouth South Town-London through trains	67
M&GNJR loco. No. 89	98
LNER loco. No. 1518E	89
N&SJRC Sign	102
BR loco. No. 61043	105